# THE NORMAN WAIT HARRIS
# MEMORIAL FOUNDATION

THE Harris Foundation Lectures at the University of Chicago have been made possible through the generosity of the heirs of Norman Wait Harris and Emma Gale Harris, who donated to the University a fund to be known as "The Norman Wait Harris Memorial Foundation" on January 27, 1923. The letter of gift contains the following statement:

> It is apparent that a knowledge of world-affairs was never of more importance to Americans than today. The spirit of distrust which pervades the Old World is not without its effect upon our own country. How to combat this disintegrating tendency is a problem worthy of the most serious thought. Perhaps one of the best methods is the promotion of a better understanding of other nations through wisely directed educational effort.
>
> The purpose of the foundation shall be the promotion of a better understanding on the part of American citizens of the other peoples of the world, thus establishing a basis for improved international relations and a more enlightened world-order. The aim shall always be to give accurate information, not to propagate opinion.

Annual Institutes have been held at the University of Chicago since the summer of 1924. The lectures delivered each year have been published in essentially their original form in a series of volumes of which this is the most recent.

# THE FOUNDATIONS OF A MORE STABLE WORLD ORDER

THE UNIVERSITY OF CHICAGO PRESS
CHICAGO, ILLINOIS

—

THE BAKER & TAYLOR COMPANY
NEW YORK

THE CAMBRIDGE UNIVERSITY PRESS
LONDON

THE MARUZEN-KABUSHIKI-KAISHA
TOKYO, OSAKA, KYOTO, FUKUOKA, SENDAI

THE COMMERCIAL PRESS, LIMITED
SHANGHAI

[Lectures on the Harris Foundation 1940]

# THE FOUNDATIONS OF A MORE STABLE WORLD ORDER

*by*

Ferdinand Schevill, *Nonresident Professor of Modern History, The University of Chicago;* Jacob Viner, *Professor of Economics, The University of Chicago;* Charles C. Colby, *Professor of Geography, The University of Chicago;* Quincy Wright, *Professor of International Law, The University of Chicago;* J. Fred Rippy, *Professor of American History, The University of Chicago;* Walter H. C. Laves, *Associate Professor of Political Science, The University of Chicago*

Walter H. C. Laves, *Editor*

THE UNIVERSITY OF CHICAGO PRESS
CHICAGO · ILLINOIS

COMPOSED AND PRINTED BY THE UNIVERSITY OF CHICAGO PRESS
CHICAGO, ILLINOIS, U.S.A.

# PREFACE

THE Norman Wait Harris Foundation was created in 1923 for the purpose of promoting a "better understanding on the part of American citizens of the other peoples of the world, thus establishing a basis for improved international relations and a more enlightened world-order." In the course of the years which have elapsed, fifteen institutes have been held at the University of Chicago on a wide variety of problems and issues, which were considered of importance to the maintenance of peace and stability in the world order of 1920–39.

The collapse of peace and the actual outbreak of warfare confronted the Harris Foundation Committee when, in the fall of 1939, plans were being made for the Sixteenth Institute scheduled for 1940. The condition of international affairs made an institute on a relatively narrow topic similar to those previously selected appear wholly inadequate. Both the trend of events and the intention of the donors seemed to indicate a subject which would permit a taking stock of our thinking during the last twenty years in order to help prepare for the changing circumstances produced by the war. It was decided, therefore, to select the subject "The

# PREFACE

Foundations of a More Stable World Order." It was not intended that there should emerge from the Institute a blueprint for a world order or a model treaty of peace. Rather, it was hoped that the Institute might aid in a clarification of views on the long- and short-range factors involved in the achievement of greater stability in the world of nations and that it might help Americans to see what policies are indicated for this country.

As in previous years, the Institute consisted of round-table discussions and public lectures. The participants in the round tables were invited, with few exceptions, from the Middle West. Special efforts were made to assure representation from the most important groups interested in international affairs. However, owing to the inability of many to leave their work and to the scheduling of one of the national-party conventions for the same dates, the final list of participants included primarily academic persons. The latter were drawn from colleges and universities and represented most of the disciplines concerned with questions relevant to the subjects of the Institute: geography, economics, political science, sociology, history, and theology.

A word should be said concerning the scope of the lectures contained in this volume. The topics for the public lectures were selected with a view to placing the subject matter of the Institute in its proper historical perspective and to emphasize some of these factors in international relations which particularly affect the stability of the world order. No attempt was made either to cover all phases of the world order so affected or to treat exhaustively the subjects under discussion. The lectures were designed to supplement the round-table discussions and at the same time, through their presentation to a larger public audience, to invite a more general concern for the problems before the Institute. Finally, it is appropriate to remind the reader of the unsettled state of world affairs throughout the months preceding the Institute and of the extraordinary nature of the crisis facing mankind while the Institute was in progress. It was a time when no mere recital of historical facts appeared adequate, when the most permanent landmarks were fast disappearing, and when speculation concerning policies for the future seemed hazardous. These conditions are reflected in the tentative nature of the following lectures and must be taken into account by the reader.

## PUBLIC LECTURES

### (Leon Mandel Hall)

I. Tuesday, June 25, 8:30 P.M.—"Can Our Civilization Achieve a More Stable World Order?" FERDINAND SCHEVILL

# PREFACE

II. Wednesday, June 26, 4:45 P.M.—"International Economic Relations and the World Order." JACOB VINER

III. Thursday, June 27, 4:45 P.M.—"The Role of Shipping in the World Order." CHARLES C. COLBY

IV. Friday, June 28, 4:45 P.M.—"International Law and the World Order." QUINCY WRIGHT

V. Monday, July 1, 4:45 P.M.—"The United States and World Order." J. FRED RIPPY

VI. Tuesday, July 2, 4:45 P.M.—"The Institutional Requirements for a More Stable World Order." WALTER H. C. LAVES

## ROUND-TABLE CONFERENCES

### (Judson Court)

I. "Causes for the Failure of the Peace of 1920"
Wednesday, June 26, 2:00 and 7:30 P.M.

*Plenary Session*—Thursday, June 27, 2:00 P.M.

II. "The Nature of Peace and War in Contemporary International Society"
Thursday, June 27, 7:30 P.M.

III. "The Institutional Framework for a More Stable World Order"
Friday, June 28, 2:00 P.M.

*Plenary Session*—Friday, June 28, 7:30 P.M.

IV. "The Role of the United States"
Monday, July 1, 2:00 and 7:30 P.M.
Tuesday, July 2, 2:00 P.M.

*Plenary Closing Session*—Tuesday, July 2, 7:30 P.M.

# PREFACE

ROUND TABLE NO. I

Chairman: Ernest B. Price, Director, International House, Chicago

Reporter: Shepherd L. Witman, Municipal University of Omaha

Harris Foundation Committee Representative: Quincy Wright

ROUND TABLE NO. II

Chairman: James K. Pollock, University of Michigan (June 25–30); Francis O. Wilcox, University of Louisville (July 1 and 2)

Reporter: Vernon Van Dyke, DePauw University

Harris Foundation Committee Representative: Robert S. Platt

ROUND TABLE NO. III

Chairman: Clifton M. Utley, Director, Chicago Council on Foreign Relations

Reporter: Franklin D. Scott, Northwestern University

Harris Foundation Committee Representative: Herbert Blumer

WALTER H. C. LAVES, *Editor*

UNIVERSITY OF CHICAGO
August 1940

# TABLE OF CONTENTS

〚 xiii 〛

# CAN OUR CIVILIZATION ACHIEVE A MORE STABLE WORLD ORDER?

*By* Ferdinand Schevill
Nonresident Professor of Modern History

# CAN OUR CIVILIZATION ACHIEVE A
# MORE STABLE WORLD ORDER?

I SHALL begin by asking you to banish from
your minds, even though only for a few brief
moments, the tremendous present happenings
that jam the foreground of your consciousness. I
am asking this in order to have you clear the way
for as unobstructed a view as possible down the
long line of march that has brought our civilization to its present pass. It is not an unreasonable
request, since it is made with the sole purpose of
coming in this manner to a better understanding
of the very events which possess us so entirely. For
what are they, what can they be other than the
last effects of a development reaching back for generations to the very beginning of our vaunted
Western civilization? Of this masterful and encom-
passing civilization everything that has happened
in its remote as in its recent past is a direct outflow
and integrated product. Every event occurring
with each new day in the seemingly diverse but
closely interlocked realms of politics, economics,
finance, international relations, religion, philosophy, literature, and the arts falls inescapably within its embrace. It is the framework of our life from

hour to hour; it is the world wherein we breathe and have our being.

In this persuasion of the organic character of our Western civilization and of its dominance over all our concerns I propose to sketch the main phases of its evolution to the end of extracting from my survey some sort of answer to the question that, for every person capable of reflection, looms behind the breathless crisis of the hour: Is a succession of world wars the inevitable concluding phase of our civilization or is there any reasonable ground for the hope, which alone lightens our present gloom, that an escape from the current international chaos into a world offering at least a measure of peace, well-being, and security is not beyond the range of possibility?

When I was a young man, half a century ago, world history was conceived and taught as a succession of world empires. The oriental empires of the Nile and Euphrates valleys headed the list. They were followed by the Mediterranean empires of Greece and Rome which, on their demise, were succeeded by the great empires of medieval and modern Europe. Within the living generation this manner of looking at world history has been effectively challenged. The concept "civilization" has won general acceptance as involving a more valid and meaningful unit of human creative activity than so purely political an institution as an empire;

and the result has been that history at the present day is largely, and, as I think, with immense profit to our sense of values, concerned with the content of those complex and loftiest products of man's adventuring spirit called civilizations.

In these circumstances the present-day historian faces as his initial task the mapping of civilizations through the ages. And the first surprise awaiting him is perhaps this—that civilizations represent peaks of achievement to which man has only rarely attained. For, while those near relatives of the historians, the anthropologists, have isolated and described literally hundreds of primitive cultures, among dead and living, the historians, pursuing their particular quest, have not been able to discover more than approximately twenty-five instances throughout the course of human history in which a primitive culture has expanded into a sufficiently fruitful expression of man's struggle with himself and his environment to merit the name of civilization.

While it would be an interesting undertaking to try to determine at exactly what point and through what a succession of influences a primitive culture is brought to abandon its strict customary norms and, animated by a new energy, to expand into a civilization, that inquiry will have to be put aside as unrelated to our purpose. We are concerned here not with primitive cultures but with civilizations and specifically with our own Western civilization. However, to establish for this civilization its proper setting within world history, we should under no circumstances fail to observe that, although a separate and unique growth, it takes its place in a succession of over a score of other civilizations, equally separate and unique. Of these other civilizations some unfolded, flowered, and died before our Western civilization came to birth; others again have very definitely run their course as its rivals and contemporaries. To the former group, you need hardly be reminded, belong the Egyptian, the Babylonian, the Greco-Roman civilizations in the eastern hemisphere, and the recently discovered Maian civilization in the western hemisphere. They have all perished from the earth, and, if we would know their drift and quality, we are obliged laboriously to reconstruct them from the scattered fragments they have left behind.

On the other hand, in such civilizations as the Hindu, the Chinese, and the Arabic we hail expressions substantially coeval with our own. They arouse our lively interest and, for some among us, exercise the fascination ever present in the unusual and mysterious. But at the same time they leave no doubt whatever in our minds that they are the product of a spirit and an attitude very different from our own. Can the difference be accounted for as an effect of climate and other similar, more or less measurable, factors of environment? We do not know. But this we do know—and it is one of the most startling aspects of the world today— that the Arabic, Hindu, Chinese, and all civilizations whatever contemporary with our own have by gradual stages become so enfeebled that they are past recovery and must shortly and inevitably collapse. Far from disputing the charge, the native-born spokesmen of these cultural bodies, above all, their political and intellectual leaders, not only themselves confirm it but vehemently outdo one another in casting off their outworn heritage in order to replace it with the indiscriminately appropriated institutions and outlook of the West. If not quite today, certainly in the not very distant future, we shall be able to offer as an undisputed fact that Western civilization, having outrun all its rivals, is the only civilization left in effective operation throughout all the continents of the earth.

Without doubt we may regard this sweeping victory as a tribute to the amazing vigor as well as to a certain inherent persuasiveness of Western civilization. While it may be said to have proved itself by its survival to possess stouter legs and deeper lungs than any of its competitors, it is also true that it has exercised, and still exercises, a tremendous lure by means of its unparalleled outlay of immediate material benefits.

But at this point we face a most perplexing anomaly: our civilization, successful over its rivals beyond every reasonable expectation, far from enjoying an unimpaired sound health, is itself passing through so violent an illness that its recovery is uncertain and impels some of the more gloomily disposed physicians gathered at its bedside to prognosticate its impending doom. Nor is this possibility to be dismissed with a laugh. If some twenty-five other civilizations have arisen in the course of human history only in the end to wither and perish, is it not a reasonable assumption that ours will not live forever? The objectively minded historian will not fail to give this consideration its due weight; but, believing as he must —or he would not be a historian—in man as a free agent, he will insist that it lies with us indefinitely to postpone the fatal hour by meeting and solving the latest crisis that confronts us exactly as we have met and solved its innumerable predecessors.

A final reflection pertinent to this coming and going of civilizations deserves to be set down. Even should our Western civilization at some unknown milestone of the future reach the end of its journey, its demise would not signify the permanent decline of man to his original primitive level.

# CAN OUR CIVILIZATION ACHIEVE IT?

In his long sojourn on earth *homo sapiens* has disclosed himself to be both a hardy and an ingenious animal, and the unceasing struggle that has characterized him to lift himself to a higher than the animal plane offers the assurance that, long before Western civilization has made its exit, he will in his undaunted way have begun a fresh cultural venture at some as yet undisclosed point of the earth's surface. For the historian of civilizations, man's works vanish, man remains.

Concentrating, after these perhaps overlong introductory remarks, on Western civilization, we note that, as in the case of all civilizations without exception, our civilization started with a vital and energizing faith. This was Christianity, defined and administered by an institution called the church. Since both faith and church were of divine origin, they constituted an irrefutable and undebatable whole. The core of Christian doctrine was that this earth, our seeming home, was a transitory and contemptible abode and that our true home was the heaven of the saints and angels which received the believer with hallelujahs at the close of his earthly trials.

It will always remain an occasion for surprise that so rarefied and transcendental a faith exercised during several centuries of the early Middle Ages a practically unchallenged authority. For, regardless of what the church taught, man could

not be genuinely persuaded to despise an earth
that generously gave him wood and stone for his
house, pasture for his cattle, and soil for his daily
bread. Every day he lived, in the Middle Ages not
otherwise than at present, he spun a thread between himself and his natural environment that
bound him to it with affectionate compulsion.
There existed therefore a disturbing contradiction
between the official and the actual convictions of
medieval men. Although it might for an indefinite
time remain unnoticed and submerged, it would
be bound ultimately to rise to the level of consciousness and call for an adjustment.

The ensuing conflict may in an abbreviated review like this be called the first great crisis of
Western civilization. After a long and heated debate it found its solution in an important reformu-
lation of Christian doctrine. The episode belongs
to the thirteenth century and was dominated by
the great scholastics, among whom St. Thomas
Aquinas stands out as the undisputed leader.
Without abating by a jot a single essential Christian teaching, St. Thomas in a simple, common-
sense sort of way made room in his system for the
earth with its diverse services to life and for man
with his bodily functions and indispensable activities. The concession, translated to the intellectual
plane, signified an endorsement of human reason
or intelligence. So high a rating was conceded by

St. Thomas to this factor that he welcomed reason as the right arm of faith and effectively utilized it to endow the Christian church with the logical underpinning it had hitherto lacked. By the labor of the scholastics, Christianity, resting originally on faith alone, gained the support of reason; and faith and reason, acting co-operatively, were conceived by their teamwork to have doubled Christianity's strength.

The most characteristic feature of a civilization as distinguished from a repetitive, primitive culture is movement. No sooner has one position been reached than another is envisaged, and preparations are begun to reach the new goal. While it is true that civilizations in their youth are conservative and therefore relatively static, there is a tendency for their pace to accelerate until in the later stages it may become so swift and dizzy as to threaten disintegration and disaster. With the scholastic compromise of the thirteenth century the cake of medieval custom began to break up more quickly than had hitherto been the case; and of course the breaking-up took place not only, or even primarily, because reason had been admitted into the hitherto hostile circle of the clerical intelligentsia. The authentication of reason as a legitimate tool was not an act performed by scholars in a philosophic vacuum. Rather, as even a hurried examination of the facts will reveal, the considerable intellectual turmoil of Aquinas' day was but the aftermath of a profound politico-social revolution covering the century and a half before his time. This revolution had in its turn resulted from the revival of commerce and the rise of towns which began around the year of our Lord 1000 and can here be no more than recalled to your minds as a familiar historical event. But what may under no circumstances be overlooked is the connection between the two medieval revolutions occurring respectively in the politico-social and the philosophic realm. Their self-evident interaction affords an excellent opportunity for insisting anew on the unity of Western civilization and the close dovetailing at all times of all its constitutive areas.

Although the thirteenth-century adjustment between faith and reason was heralded by its proponents as an arrangement valid for all eternity, before a generation had passed it was challenged by that very "reason" which the scholastics had admitted into a partnership with faith. True, they had not done so without first cutting its claws, so to speak, by ascribing to it a definite, strictly circumscribed function. But, unhappily for the scholastic plan, the claws grew again and, reasserting its untamed nature, "reason" was soon breaking into any garden that tempted its curiosity, no matter how well set around with ecclesiastical warnings to keep out.

And, once again, this disconcerting boldness was not an isolated inspiration of the body of intellectuals. The intellectuals were no more than a handful of men in a vast societal complex engaged in carrying forward the revolution connected with the towns and the formation of an enterprising body of town residents. By the fourteenth and fifteenth centuries the movement had brought Western civilization to the notable milestone inscribed with the name of the Renaissance.

The Renaissance phase of Western civilization had its start in Italy for reasons that reveal themselves at a glance to even the casual investigator. In commerce, finance, and industry Italy was at that time by far the most advanced country of the West. Emboldened by their astounding economic successes, the Italians thereupon led the way in setting aside the medieval religious limitations and in making a constantly increasing use of that "reason" or free intelligence to which the scholastic philosophers had given their solemn sanction. Consequently, it was these same Italians who first championed the return to antiquity called the "Revival of Learning." They brought the ancient learning back to life and proposed to bury under it the outmoded scholastic learning of the Middle Ages. In their heated pursuit of this aim they revived such pagan philosophies as Stoicism and Epicureanism, lifting them as proposed ways of living to a position of honor at the side of Christianity. And, doubtless their most memorable achievement, they gave an amazingly rich expression, above all, in painting and sculpture, to their fresh and enlarged world of thought and feeling. While we note, perhaps not without surprise, that the Renaissance sculptors and painters contented themselves in the main with the subject matter of the Madonna and the saints inherited from their predecessors, they gave it a nonmedieval, and even an antimedieval, character by steeping it in the vivid natural world about them to which their eyes had been joyously opened.

From Italy the Renaissance made its way by slow stages over the rest of Europe, not because the rest of Europe was pleased to play the ape to Italy, but because it, too, was being reshaped by the same urban movement that had already sown the Italian lands with prosperous towns. To some apprehensive souls of that age it may have looked as if the old pagan gods were returning from their graves to displace the Christian saints and martyrs who a thousand years before had displaced them. It was a false alarm. Christianity was not to be so easily uprooted from the minds and hearts of men. The too rapid spread of the Renaissance liberties, joined to the affront they signified to long-established custom, produced a reaction that came to a thundering head in the Reformation. The Reformation was a reassertion of Christianity against a threatening paganism; and it was just that in no less degree because it was also a revolt against the ancient Christian church. For this ancient church had, at its official summit in Italy, at Rome, become identified with the Renaissance, and by reason of this taint had aroused the unbridled wrath of the Protestant dissenters and removed itself for them outside the Christian pale.

Limitations imposed by the ground I have set myself to cover oblige me to indicate the further development of Western civilization with a few shorthand symbols. In the nick of time and with hardly a moment to spare the diminished Roman Catholic church cut itself loose from the Renaissance and re-established contact with its imposing medieval past by matching the Protestant Reformation with a Reformation of its own. Therewith we have the phase of Western civilization which followed on the heels of the Renaissance. It carries the label "Reformation versus Counter-Reformation" and is a period of religious disturbance wherein two, and, finally, more than half-a-dozen, interpretations of Christianity disputed with one another possession of the Western lands and peoples.

By the middle of the seventeenth century, by the time, let us say, of the Treaty of Westphalia, the religious exaltation, inaugurated a hundred years before by the Protestant revolt, began to subside and has, with an occasional interruption, continued to subside ever since. And lo and behold, in measure, as religion relaxed its grip on the Western mind, the seemingly crushed spirit of the Renaissance again raised its head. It had really never been crushed; it had only gone into hiding to await the passing of the storm. For, sincere as both Reformation and Counter-Reformation were in their purpose again to make religion the prime concern of life, they were unable to win acceptance for the doctrine, or rather total attitude, of other-worldliness, which is the original Christian essence. Ever since the upheaval begun by the rise of the towns, which is of such central significance for the line of travel followed by our civilization, European man has devoted himself with increasing energy to the reduction of this earth of ours to his service. By thus committing himself he had, in the Christian sense of the word, become worldly; and not even so powerful, so tidal a wave of religious revival as the Reformation interlude could again wean him from his mundane frame of mind.

If this statement should seem to be extravagant, abundant evidence in its support can be adduced from the Reformation period itself, when the religious issue occupied so large a segment of human consciousness. Never for a moment during that period was the pursuit of secular activities inaugurated during the Renaissance abandoned. Rather it was intensified in a score of different directions. The already far-flung network of commerce led to undertakings of wider and ever wider range. They culminated at last in the voyages of discovery by which Africa, Asia, and the Americas were brought within the reach of Europe and subjected to European exploitation. Surely a more conclusive renunciation of Christian other-worldliness than this passionate appropriation of the earth cannot be imagined.

And in a society of closely interwoven parts the voyages of discovery were of necessity but a link in an unbroken chain of events. By their sensational success they redoubled the spirit of enterprise in which they had originated. The large-scale business transactions that followed necessitated correspondingly large-scale financial measures. The use of money, in place of barter, spread even to the outlying corners of Europe; and accumulated savings, put at the disposal of merchants and manufacturers, laid the solid groundwork of modern capitalism. The wealth of great cities, especially of maritime cities, registered an uninterrupted increase, and the employment of that wealth by bankers, shipbuilders, company promoters, and enterprisers of every kind gradually impressed that bourgeois or middle-class character on society which it has substantially kept down to our day.

Nor could the mounting importance of the new urban group fail to affect the central government. It was the pressure of the bourgeoisie that brought about that strengthening of the royal authority at the expense of the hitherto dominant land-lord or feudal class that figures in history as the rise of the national monarchy. Not till the Reformation, let us recall, did the national monarchies of Spain, France, and England begin to tower like giants over Europe and give shape to that power system which still exercises an unbroken sway. The several versions of Christianity that fought so furiously for supremacy during the Reformation may have deluded themselves with the idea that as soon as they had reached an accommodation they would divide the rule of Europe among them. To such dreamers the Treaty of Westphalia must have been a cruel awakening. For by the middle of the seventeenth century a man would have had to be staring blind not to be overwhelmed with the evidence that henceforth the development of Europe was going to revolve, primarily, not around religion but around the newly risen, self-conscious nation.

With the advent on the scene of the political novelty, the nation, we have arrived at the consideration of the most recent phase of Western civilization. A minute analyst would, of course, not find it difficult to distinguish a number of subtly differentiated subphases of development between the Reformation and the present day. However, for the survey purposes of this exposition, the movement of the last three hundred years may without injury to the facts be designated as a single phase. And again, with no more than a bird's-eye view in mind, the statement may be ventured that one other factor has co-operated with the national state as a main determinant of the character of Western civilization in this most recent period of its unfolding. That other factor is science or rationalism. To equate science and rationalism may at first blush seem questionable but will presently and, I hope, convincingly be justified. In any case, the remainder of this paper will be concerned with setting forth the part played by the nation-state and by science in giving our civilization its current shape and burdening it with its current problems.

Of the nation-state, I have already said, and now repeat, that it made its appearance in the form of a monarchy, and specifically of the French monarchy, the Spanish monarchy, and the English monarchy. The historical circumstances that conspired to bring these three national monarchies into existence are so well known that there is no need of recounting them, aside from pointing out that the king was in each instance already in existence and that the new and steadily mounting social element, the middle class, found it convenient to throw its support to him against its bitter class enemies, the nobility. Although the king owed much of the re-spect with which he was regarded to the public services he rendered in his capacity of chief executive, the awed reverence, which re-enforced the respect, sprang from his being the visible embodiment and symbol of the nation. For a considerable time after his rise the national monarch was more or less of an absolute monarch and hedged about with a divinity that enveloped him like an aureole.

Thus matters stood for several generations during which the bourgeois backers of the monarch gained a constantly increasing importance. Should it happen, in the altered circumstances, that the king forgot he served the nation in general and the middle class in particular, his divinity speedily evaporated and he himself was either driven into exile or dragged like a criminal to the scaffold. In no case known to history was the nation-state enfeebled in its might or altered in its essential character by the deposition of a king who failed to grasp his historical mission. What commonly happened on his elimination was that the victorious bourgeoisie took over the power directly and made up for the loss of the sovereign's emblematic value by substituting for him such broadly equivalent symbols as president of the republic, the national flag, and the national anthem.

Belatedly, because not until the nineteenth century, did the central European peoples—the Italians and Germans—and their small southeastern neighbors of the Balkan Peninsula organize them selves as national states. When, following the First World War, half a score of minor peoples incorporated in the nationally mixed Austrian and Russian empires followed suit, the principle of nationality may be said to have completed its sweep of the European continent. Long before this event the nation-state had triumphed in the Americas; and, as a final evidence of its infectious vitality, we may note that it has at the present time gained at least a foothold in all the other continents of the earth.

How is the amazing, world-circling victory of nationalism to be explained? On the most immediate level, that of sentiment, the answer is simple and unchallengeable: nationalism is the strongest emotional force in the world today through which the individual is able to transcend his ephemeral self and to become identified with the relative permanence of a self-perpetuating group. In the Middle Ages religion fulfilled this function of animating its followers with an irrational fervor for a cause beyond their little lives. Medieval men died willingly to carry their faith and its promise of salvation to the unenlightened heathen. When, in the seventeenth century, religion's last bid for control failed, something had to be found to take its place; for, as from the time the world began, men are still prompted to supreme, self-sacrificing action not by deliberate cerebration but by the unreflecting movement of the heart. That something which on its enfeeblement replaced religion turned out to be the nation-state, and the fact is spread in such bold streamers across the pages of history that there is no need to assemble instances.

Now, since the lives of men, if they are to be lived with even a small measure of satisfying conviction, cannot dispense with an emotional content, and since, all around the globe, that content has through a development which cannot be reversed become an unreasoned and instinctive attachment to a land, a group, a people, it would be psychologically and historically absurd to quarrel with nationalism in itself. But our acceptance of it as a force legitimately here and at work among us is no reason for failing to observe a tendency which it shares with emotions and states of mind that at other times have taken possession of mankind. Something apparently native to our species impels it to push a development and to pursue a conviction to the utmost limit until it at last breaks down of its own weight. As far back as the days of the Greeks, the great Aristotle raised his voice in warning against this human, all too human, trend. He and countless sages since his time have urged measure in all things as man's best guide through the mazes of existence. But the actual practice of man has not been measure; it has been excess to the point of breakdown.

Applying this observation to the development of nationalism, we note that even while it was girdling the globe and making itself universal, it was also becoming ever more heedless and inflamed. If, during the nineteenth century, it still submitted on occasion to the check of reason and the common good, with the twentieth century it began to cast aside every restraining influence and to act as if it recognized no law but its own. The climax of this development is the bewildering current phenomenon of totalitarianism.

So much attention has been accorded to what may be called the fringes of totalitarian doctrine that we seem sometimes to be in danger of not seeing the wood for the trees. To this blindness the totalitarian spokesmen have contributed by proclaiming in and out of season a social program with so many elements arousing not only criticism but also instinctive resentment that attention has been diverted from the totalitarian core. Among these programmatic elements on which criticism has been quick to fasten are such matters as economic self-sufficiency, reckless population increase, and Aryan superiority coupled with anti-Semitism.

While these and similar propositions are objects of legitimate attack, small headway is made against them unless it is always remembered that they are nothing but the by-products of a single and absolutely central doctrine. And that is nationalism or, if you prefer, extreme or ultra-nationalism. There is therefore nothing essentially new about the totalitarian state. Its kernel has been with us ever since the rise of the national monarchy three hundred years ago. We come closest to an understanding of it if we accept it as the latest shape of that nation-state which by the twentieth century had made its way into every corner of the earth. The totalitarian state is the nation-state carried, in accordance with a psychological law that apparently rules human behavior, to its excess and breaking-point.

Let us now turn to the second agency which, according to the opinion of this reviewer, has co-operated with the nation-state to give our civilization its present decisive aspects. That agency is science, which, in the perspective of its origin, may be confidently bracketed with human reason. After first asserting itself in the scholastic period, and still more emphatically in the subsequent Renaissance, reason was again smothered by the religious interests that burst irrepressibly to the front with the Reformation. Then, when, around the middle of the seventeenth century, Reformation and Counter-Reformation had spent their force, reason came once again to the fore and quickly acquired an ascendancy in the intellectual realm from which it has never again been driven.

It was of course only that limited segment of Western humanity called the intelligentsia that identified itself with reason and confidently set it to work. But, having set it to work, the intelligentsia was confirmed in its decision by the most considerable conquest attributable to reason throughout all the ages of man—the conquest of science. Or, with the view to reducing the immense world of science to its simplest communicable form, let us rather say that what the followers of rational procedure achieved in the seventeenth century was a novel and, as it turned out, unbelievably fruitful scientific method.

It would be an unjustifiable departure from our main purpose to describe in detail the scientific method which received its first formulation from a line of physical scientists extending from Copernicus to Newton. Nor, fortunately, is a description at all necessary in the case of an academic audience such as is here assembled. Suffice it to point out that the method devised in the first instance for the field of physics was found valid for every other division of science, and that there has resulted from this widened application a steadily deepening knowledge of the world of nature.

In view of this unexampled success, it was inevitable that in the course of time the demand should have made itself heard that the studies concerned with the world of man should adopt the same method, thereby raising themselves from haphazard social studies to the rank of social sciences. Impressed by this intention, our American universities have very generally within the last two decades clapped this solemn nomenclature on the studies concerned with man; but nobody knows better than the incumbents of the social chairs that their studies are still so erratic and fallible that to label them sciences is an open invitation to ridicule.

But the lag of the misnamed social sciences is no fault of the scientific method developed, as we have noted, not for them but for the world of nature. Therefore, no subtraction whatever need be made from the statement already ventured that scientific method, together with the mountain of tested knowledge it has accumulated, has dominated the intellectual world for the last three hundred years.

Indirectly, if not directly, science and scientific method have also dominated the much wider, non-intellectual world of average men. They have been able to extend their rule in this manner by means of those enthusiastically welcomed and fondly cherished by-products of science, our innumerable modern inventions. Need it be specially pointed out that it was through them, and not through science considered in itself, that Western civilization has experienced the most profound alteration in its structure during its whole long history? We call this structural transformation the Industrial Revolution and note with pride, not unmixed at this later hour with serious misgivings, that, inaugurated several generations ago, it has steadily gained momentum until now it sweeps us forward into the dark and unpredictable future at a breath-taking pace.

In these circumstances our runaway Industrial Revolution may without hesitation be adduced as another example of man's tendency to carry a movement to excess, to strain an idea, valuable in itself, to the breaking-point. But whether this tendency be accepted or rejected as a general psychological law, no one giving serious consideration to our present plight will fail to agree that we are afflicted with both an international and a domestic chaos, attributable in last analysis to an abusive exaggeration of the two ruling forces of our civilization—science and the nation-state. And a fact absolutely central to every diagnosis undertaken with a view to an eventual cure is that these two agencies have enjoyed and still enjoy our enthusiastic endorsement. You will search in vain throughout the Western world for any sizable, organized group prepared to renounce either scientific method or the national idea. Lacking an obsessive religion, the Western peoples are unwilling to give up the emotional substitute of nationalism; and, having experienced the benefits resulting from the unhampered use of the intelligence, they yield an unqualified devotion to science and the unnumbered material blessings it has lavished upon them.

Nonetheless, a rapidly increasing number of individuals, alarmed by the uninterrupted spread of international and industrial disorder, have in recent years been assailed by doubts regarding our two master trends. They have suggested various corrective measures which, as a rule, do not cut very deep. In sharp contrast to them, a small group of radically inclined dissenters has with great fervor advocated a retreat from our advanced positions all the way back to the Middle Ages. In that still so generally maligned period, they point out, the ecclesiastical power was stronger than the civil power and kept, or at least tried to keep, all economic and intellectual movements within what were conceived to be socially healthy limits. While, in accordance with the organic theory touching civilizations here sustained, the return of Western civilization to a previous state is an impossible reversal of the laws of growth, it may not be doubted that it is the privilege and obligation of free agents, such as in the main we assume ourselves to be, to give the deepest consideration of which we are capable to the pruning of forces in our society that have waxed overgreat and have got out of hand.

I cannot elaborate this thesis as I should like. I can do no more than indicate a line of development along which we in the United States have recently begun to move and which in one very definite respect draws us into a kind of mental sympathy with the Middle Ages. The Middle Ages, bowing in willing submission to an accepted divine law, worked out a concordant ethical code of a social and community character. This code the Protestant Reformation replaced with an individualist and libertarian code on which the whole social, political, and mental development of the post-Reformation centuries has been predicated.

It is not only enthusiasts of the Middle Ages but also extremely modern and anything but medievally minded economists, sociologists, and philosophers who have recently raised their voices in favor of replacing our chaotic society, composed of individual atoms engaged in a ferocious struggle for survival, with a society operated for the common good according to a plan inspired by a socially oriented moral code. If such a revolution is ever to be brought about, an indispensable preliminary measure would have to be the surrender of our inherited individualist ethics that raises the individual above society and the substitution therefor of a social ethics that merges and submerges him in the group.

And such an exchange, if ever effected, might not without justice be described as a return to the Middle Ages.

I hope no one in my audience was drawn here to-night on the naïve assumption that I was going to answer the question raised by my title: Can Our Civilization Achieve a More Stable World Order? The mere proposal on the part of a single, puny mortal to divert from its course the river of Time would constitute an act of such monumental presumption that whatever gods may still be sitting enthroned on high Olympus would at once bury it beneath their inextinguishable laughter. If our civilization is to be given another shape, if it is to achieve even a slight measure of stability in place of its present perilous instability, that will have to be the work not of a feeble, isolated critic or, under the rationalism prevailing in our society, of a God-intoxicated prophet crying in the wilderness but of purposefully organized groups around the world seeking a common understanding and moving forward with unshaken resolution to their visioned goal.

Wherewith we have arrived at the Sixteenth Institute of the Harris Foundation, which is opening its sessions today. The committee in charge has mapped out a program of lectures and round-table conferences which is in your hands and which lists for discussion some of the more immediately pressing issues involved in a better world order. We are going to try to get light for our guidance from the failure of the treaties of 1919 and of the League of Nations woven with them into an inseparable coil. We shall explore the nature of peace and war in a shrunken world of economically, technically, and culturally interdependent nation-states. We shall try to discover the minimum institutional requirements indispensable to a truly effective international order.

Thus engaged, we shall be doing what Institutes similarly inspired have done before us and what we may hope a long succession of other Institutes will continue to do in the future. The issues involved in a more stable world order are, as everybody is only too keenly aware, enormously difficult and incredibly complicated. The Institute realizes that the first need is for them to be analyzed and clarified by the co-operative labors of many kinds of specialists extending over many years. On being gradually reduced by digestion and redigestion to simple, communicable terms, they will then have to be spread around the globe by the written and the spoken word until they are the property everywhere of the common run of mankind. For, if the new world order for which we are trying to prepare the way is to be something more than an academic dream, if it is ever to take substantial form among us, it will have to rest not on the resolutions of an intelligentsia, no matter how generously inspired, but on a world opinion deepened to a world conviction and elevated to a world faith.

However, the discussions we are about to begin of the issues and forces occupying the immediate foreground of the international situation can only at the risk of nullifying our own findings neglect the background out of which the foreground factors have historically emerged. I close therefore as I began by asserting that the present age constitutes the latest phase of Western civilization, which has evolved organically through a thousand-year span in a succession of closely interlocked phases. The current phase is ruled by science and the nation-state, from which consequently the leading aspects as well as the leading problems of our time necessarily stem. Although neither one nor the other of these dominants is expressly mentioned in the Institute's agenda, they are both of them implicit in every subject listed for discussion. It follows that unless we remain alertly aware of the deep historical roots of the various heads of debate and, further, that unless we remain mindful that our civilization is a unique growth constituting a matrix which masterfully conditions our development we shall run the risk of merely scratching the surface of our problems instead of probing to their heart and core.

# INTERNATIONAL ECONOMIC RELATIONS
# AND THE WORLD ORDER

*By* JACOB VINER
Professor of Economics

# INTERNATIONAL ECONOMIC RELATIONS AND THE WORLD ORDER

APPROPRIATELY enough, I suppose, for an Institute devoted to the promotion of a beneficent world order, the topic assigned to me today is "International Economic Relations and the World Order." I must confess, however, that today topics relating to the "world order" have for me a somewhat antiquarian and unreal flavor. But I will try to be a good soldier and to adhere to my assignment, at least for a time.

It has for many years been the belief of many economists, and of some other persons, that the minimization of national barriers to international trade and to international economic relations in general would promote international peace—not would guarantee international peace, but would contribute to international peace—and that it would do so in the following ways:

It would operate to remove economic sources of international friction. By furthering the prosperity of the countries engaged in international economic co-operation, it would relieve internal tensions and would thus lessen the tendency for such countries to find relief from internal troubles in international adventures. By promoting the mutual dependence of nations it would increase their vulnerability, military as well as economic, in time of war and would also increase the economic losses consequent upon lack of success in war and thus, for prudential reasons, would promote a pacific attitude. What I have in mind here is that if countries, because of a free-trade policy, had become seriously dependent on outside sources for their essential supplies of foodstuffs and raw materials, if their industries had become specialized to the supply of certain export markets, if these industries could not readily be shifted to war objectives or to production for the domestic market, then there would be important prudential considerations leading these countries toward the maintenance of friendly international relations or at least toward the avoidance of war.

There is an additional argument for free trade as promotive of peace which has the support of a good deal of authoritative opinion but to which I am inclined to attach very little weight. This is the argument that the international contacts which the conduct of international trade promotes, as between individuals and groups, themselves lead to international good will and understanding. I have a suspicion that the contrary may be nearer the truth.

I do, however, attach a substantial amount of weight to the first three considerations I have enumerated. I believe that they do have considerable validity. But I believe also that some enthusiasts, and particularly the Cobden-Bright School and their followers, have exaggerated the importance of economic factors in determining the state of international relations, and especially that they have exaggerated the efficacy of a free-trade policy in promoting international peace.

When England, in the period from about 1846 until the end of the century, did follow a policy of almost complete nondiscrimination between British and non-British economic interests, many writers, both Continental and American, instead of interpreting it as a generous policy, as a policy of international economic co-operation, or as a policy which at least demonstrated the absence of aggressive purposes on the part of England, gave it a counterinterpretation. They interpreted, or pretended to interpret, the English free-trade policy and practice as part of a deep-laid and villainous scheme of England to obtain economic mastery over the rest of the world. They said that England was ahead of other countries in its industrial development, that England therefore had nothing to fear from foreign competition from any direction (which, in the sense which they gave to it, is an absurd proposition), and that the adoption by England of free trade was a deliberate trap that she had set to entice other countries to follow suit and thus to obtain the destruction of their economic defenses against English industrial supremacy and to make them helpless victims of English economic and political imperialistic designs. Typical of a substantial literature of the period, on the Continent and in the United States, was a book published in 1878 whose title, as translated from the original French, "The Enormities of English Free Trade,"[1] correctly indicates the character of its argument.

Where there exist any factors, whether psychological or political or economic, leading to international enmity, the reasons to be used explicitly in justifying such enmity can readily be manufactured or found in almost any direction. The very activities of one country which may be intended to promote peace and should have this effect, such as the removal of trade barriers, may be made—have been made—by other countries the pretext for preparation for war or for the pursuit of policies conducive to war.

I accept the thesis that freer trade is on the whole conducive to peace. But, in the light of past experience, I think it wise to guard against attributing great efficacy to it. In any case, the world has as a whole since the 1880's moved definitely and at an accelerating pace away from commitment

[1] J. Borain, *Les Enormités du libre èchange anglais* (Bruxelles, 1878).

both to freer trade and to peace. I cannot attempt a complete explanation of why the world has moved away from free trade, counter to the advice of economists for the larger part, and especially of English and American economists. But certain factors that have been operative in this direction can readily be identified.

The tariff, it has been said, is not like a coat which you can put on when the weather turns a little bit brisk and take off when the sun comes out, but is rather like a coat of skin and feathers which is acquired painlessly and slowly and unconsciously but, once you have it, can be gotten rid of only at the cost of blood and pain. There are heavy, short-time costs, especially during periods of unemployed resources, in getting rid of long-existent trade barriers. There are also special interests in the maintenance of or in the addition to the structure of trade barriers, and these tend to be more concentrated and therefore more alert and more vigorous in exerting political pressure than the special, and especially than the general, interests which also exist in the removal of existing barriers and in the abstinence from the erection of new ones.

Also, there has been failure on the part of the economists, except for a fairly substantial period in England—and to me a somewhat miraculous period—to convert the public to the general principle of free trade, even in principle. There has been general agreement, moreover, even among free-trade economists, that multilateral reduction of trade barriers is more beneficial than unilateral reduction of trade barriers. Even economists have therefore counseled that the removal of trade barriers wait upon the negotiation of successful bilateral or multilateral agreements, which would remove them simultaneously in a number of countries, thus giving assurance that when you remove a barrier to the inflow of goods into your market, you at the same time obtain removal of a foreign barrier to the outflow of your goods. The task of obtaining multilateral action toward the reduction of trade barriers has unfortunately proved to be one which calls for more zeal on the part of statesmen and more skill in diplomacy and in the technical task of administering conferences than has been available.

Finally, and probably of little importance, there has been sabotage among the economists themselves of the case for free trade. They have overdeveloped theoretical paradoxes and subtleties which point to the possibility under certain limited assumptions that trade barriers might yield a net national profit or might even promote trade, while failing to stress or playing down the major issue as it faced the public, namely, do trade barriers, in the form and degree in which they already exist or are likely to be established, promote or injure the national economic welfare? The somewhat divided counsels which have prevailed among economists on this issue must of course in the main be attributed to genuine differences of belief. There have been instances, also, when, because of party affiliations or because of the acceptance of non-economic national objectives, economists who have accepted in principle the economic argument for free trade have been unable to support a policy of free trade. This was most notably the case in England in connection with the development of the so-called Imperial Federation movement, when ardent British "imperialists"—giving to that term the special meaning it has in England—were willing to accept the tariff not as an economic good in itself but as a necessary instrument toward the attainment of a greater unity of the British Empire. In the United States there have been cases where economists professionally friendly to trade-unions or to agriculture have taken over from their friends with other intellectual baggage their hostility toward free trade.

I think also that some instances of support of protectionism by individual economists can be attributed to exhibitionism. The free-trade doctrine is to economists unexciting, prosaic, routine, conventional, traditional, uninspiring. There is no distinction and no reputation for originality or intellectual daring to be derived from expounding it.

Its only virtue is that it is right. That has been, I fear, for some economists, sufficient occasion for endeavoring to find flaws in it.

If we turn to the post-war years, which were, of course, the most vital years in determining the present-day course of events, I see three critical post-war occasions when special circumstances and the special efforts of particular statesmen made it conceivable, at least to the optimist, that radical movement in the direction of freer trade—in the direction of the substantial removal of trade barriers—might possibly have been achieved; but in each case there was failure—primarily failure on the part of the statesmen participating in these activities.

The first occasion was the Treaty of Versailles and its aftermath. Here I would say the failure was not only on the part of the Treaty of Versailles itself, whatever its defects, for it froze nothing for time eternal but on the contrary contained within itself provisions making possible the remedying of anything which needed remedying. If these provisions were not adequately made use of, the fault lay not only with France and England but also with the United States because of our failure to enter the League of Nations, which was to be the instrument for promoting the desirable ends to which the Treaty of Versailles at least gave lip service, and because of our pursuit of economic policies which could breed only trouble for international relations.

The second occasion was the Geneva Economic Conference of 1927, in which we participated on the sidelines as a mildly benevolent observer, without vigor, without plan, without genuine willingness to make a contribution of our own. If the Conference failed, and failed dismally, as it did, it was at least as much because of fault on our part as because of similar fault on the part of the other major participating countries.

Finally, there was the London Economic Conference of 1933, which provided the most recent opportunity that the world has had, and the last chance I feel sure it is going to have for a very long time, to establish a sensible international economic world order. For the collapse of this Conference this country not only carries a share of the responsibility but a peculiarly heavy and to me inexplicable one.

There were also, as I read post-war history, four fatal steps in the direction of increasing and extending to new fields the already sufficiently impressive set of trade barriers. The first was the Fordney-McCumber Tariff of 1922, significant because it came at a strategic moment when the significance for the future course of history of the Treaty of Versailles and its implications and of the League of Nations and its implications was still to be determined. This step of ours was interpreted throughout the outside world as a reliable index of the economic path which the greatest, the richest, of the powers was going to follow in the post-war period. It was taken as evidence that a better world economic order, if attainable at all, would have to be constructed without hope of American co-operation.

The next fatal step was the Smoot-Hawley Tariff Act of 1930, again coming at a critical moment, because it came at the onset of a severe world depression, and made it evident that this country was going to look for relief from the very genuine and the very hard pressures of a major economic depression which American mistakes had inflicted upon the world at large as well as upon ourselves, by the further shutting-off of the American market to foreign commodities.

Finally, there were the Ottawa agreements of 1932, which constituted an important step toward making the modern British Empire, like the old British Empire of the eighteenth century, a closed empire for trade purposes, with preferential tariff treatment within the empire and high tariff barriers against the outside world.

I am inclined to add also, as another fatal step, one in which a large part of the world participated —the breakdown of the international gold standard. It was not a perfect standard. Every Freshman in economics can draw the blueprints for a better one. But it was an international standard, and as long as most of the world adhered to it there was assurance that exchange depreciation would not be used to reinforce the barriers against imports provided by tariffs. The breakdown of the gold standard made deliberate exchange depreciation available as an additional method of obstructing imports and also as an additional obstacle to the international flow of capital. It promoted the adoption of exchange controls and barter trade and of national economic planning, as defensive measures against the deflationary effect of foreign currency depreciations.

If I had been giving this lecture a year ago I suppose the main substance of my lecture would have been the significance of the Hull Trade Agreement program. This program is, I now fear, going to go down in the pages of history as a magnificent gesture but an unsuccessful one. It was an attempt, mostly a one-man attempt, to stem the tide, to go against what has proved to be the trend of history. Secretary Hull—and, I repeat, mostly by his own efforts, without anything at all approaching 100 per cent co-operation from his colleagues—did succeed at least in winning formal adherence of the United States to the principle of the desirability of the removal of trade barriers. He even succeeded in getting some actual, though slight, removal of trade barriers on our part and on the part of other countries. At the same time, however, new trade barriers were being erected by this and other governments, and Hull's success in maintaining American adherence to the principle of the desirability of the removal of trade barriers was won only at the price of making only very minor motions in the direction of their actual removal.

I am aware that I have been indulging, in accordance with good academic tradition, in remembrance of better times past, of those happier days when economists and other men of enlightenment and good will could without too obvious futility give utterance to hopes for a better-ordered world and could launch innumerable projects of reform having in common the characteristic that, although for a common-sense world they would have been prosaic and unambitious, for this very different world they were to prove hopelessly utopian. We must face the fact that history is on the march and that it is marching to a tune which we shall not easily bring ourselves cheerfully to play or to listen to. The chief lesson which examination of the history of our past efforts, when combined with a little resort to easy prophecy, can teach us is that the impending course of events is going to be very different from that which we had wished for and in our ineffective manner worked to bring about.

Though there may be little profit, however, there is a modicum of sad pleasure to be derived from contemplation of the record of wasted opportunities and of oversanguine expectations. I hope, therefore, that you will bear with me for a few more moments while, still in this nostalgic mood, I comment on the latest of the "liberal" projects for world economic reform—"federal union"—which was born too late to have a future and only not quite late enough to be stillborn. This proposal for a federal union between the democracies as a means of establishing, for at least that portion of the world which might still be persuaded to accept it, a basis for close international economic and political co-operation on democratic principles is, in Clarence Streit's and other versions thereof, sensible and well intentioned in its objectives. It takes, however, the existence of large stocks of international good will and the capacity for mutual co-operation in international affairs so much for granted that, at least now, we can see clearly (if we could not last year) that it is not of this earth, earthy, and that it is imbued with a spirit which, admirable though it be, marks it as belonging to a lost past or perhaps to a very distant future but not to the immediate present.

I think federal union a highly desirable objective and that even as late as last year it was proper to preach it. Although its chances for realization were exceedingly slim, I then saw no reason for absolute conviction on anyone's part that it could not possibly be carried into execution and could not possibly work. A year ago it seemed sensible to try to convert the democratic part of the world to the principles essential for its salvation although not sensible to be too optimistic about the chances of success. But, alas, now it is definitely too late. There aren't very many democracies remaining, and there are definitely going to be fewer. And to continue now to speak of federal union between the democracies as something still conceivably attainable is to indulge in wishful thinking and to engage in aggravated "blueprintitis." Not that I do not believe in blueprints. I believe both in blueprints that are drawn with a view to the existent probabilities and in blueprints that put on record one's daydreams. I think it wise, however, to keep them in separate mental compartments and never to mistake the one for the other. The project for federal union would have had slim chances at any time. One analogy from history frequently drawn to show that it was conceivable that you could get the world to accept that sort of proposal is it seems to me largely a false one; namely, the analogy drawn from the experience of the United States. The countries which it is now being proposed to bring into a federal union are to a large extent countries with traditions of war and of enmity, with racial and language differences, with different cultural traditions and outlooks, and with long and cherished histories of national autonomy. The American Colonies, on the other hand, were of common race and language and political and cultural traditions; they had together fought for and won their political freedom; separate, they would be weak and without prestige; united, they would at once constitute the dominant power in their hemisphere; there was available for most of them either unlimited room for peaceful territorial expansion without encroaching on one another's territory or else opportunities for territorial conquest which could be realized only through the use of the combined strength of all the Colonies. It took some time, moreover, before the separate Colonies were willing to surrender real power over the controversial issues to the central government, especially in the economic field, and later it took a civil war—the costliest one in blood and money the world perhaps has ever known—to keep the Union intact. The federal-union project calls for the surrender on the part of the participating countries of the right to maintain trade barriers against each other, but the members of this American Union, which is taken as a model, after one hundred and fifty years of union, are actively engaged in erecting trade barriers at the state boundaries, with the Supreme Court declaring its impotence and the federal Congress demonstrating its unwillingness to check the process of national economic disintegration.

Now, having done homage to the academic proprieties by what I hope was a reasonably objective historical survey and by treatment of the scholar's ideals as if they were significant, I will come down to the hard, cold, and bloody realities.

I think European union is now a real prospect—more real than it has been at least since Napoleon's time—but it will not be Clarence Streit's federal union. It will be a tighter union than that, and a more effective one, and it will have extra-European annexes. It will be a Hitlerian union. It will be imperial rather than federal—a ruling country with dependencies and satellites. If one may judge both from the indications afforded by the policy of Germany in these matters since it has become powerful and from what seem to be the inherent rationalities of the case, given the objectives and the temperament of Germany under its present rulers, it will be a union with a strong central control of economic policy, directed primarily to serve the interests, economic or otherwise, of the ruling country. It will be ruthless, it will have no moral scruples of any kind, it will be skilfully planned to attain its given objectives, and it will be efficiently administered.

What are likely to be those objectives in the

economic sphere? Prominent, I think, will be the
desire to approach fairly closely—not completely,
but fairly closely—to self-sufficiency for the controlled area for a number of reasons. Self-sufficiency facilitates central planning, and central
planning is part of the essence of—is a necessity to
—a war economy: to an aggressive, expanding,
ambitious, national economy. Self-sufficiency elimi-
nates the need for building up and maintaining
regional reserves of buying power for emergencies.
Self-sufficiency, therefore, up to a certain point,
directly contributes to military strength. It incidentally makes gold holdings a luxury, which is an
advantage for an area that has no gold.

For Continental Europe, minus Russia, I suppose, plus a few well-selected available or soon-
to-be available colonial areas, self-sufficiency would
be attainable without Spartan economies—at least
for the ruling country, especially after consumers
in the dependent areas had been disciplined to want
only what it is desired by the ruling country that
they shall want and to produce what the ruling
country had most need for. If scarcities remain
they can be overcome in large part through a continuation of the application of German technical
capacity to the task of discovery of substitutes and
of new internal sources of supply.

What would a Hitlerian Europe do with respect
to trade with other areas? For a time, I think, a

German-controlled Europe would continue to trade fairly extensively with noncontrolled areas, while it was waiting for the development of internal sources of supply of scarce materials and the discovery of fairly satisfactory substitutes. It would also engage in trade as an entering wedge for political penetration. In this connection the record of the relations of Nazi Germany with the Balkan States is quite significant, I think.

Germany's first overtures to the Balkan States for special trading arrangements on the exchange control or barter basis appeared very attractive to the Balkan countries. In the first year or two or three most of the Balkan countries were thoroughly satisfied, on the whole, with the outcome of their trade arrangements with Germany. Germany gave them pledges, which it adhered to, to take definite amounts annually of their products—a great advantage, especially during a period of world depression. It gave them good products at reasonable prices in exchange.

But gradually, as Germany made these countries more and more dependent on the German export market by taking more and more of their exports, it became a stronger and stronger bargainer. As Germany acquired control over the Czechoslovakian area and then over the Polish area its bargaining power as a buyer increased still further. It used that power with discretion and with finesse but without scruples. At the International Studies Conference which took place at Bergen, Norway, last August, it was interesting to hear one representative after another of the smaller European countries tell very much the same story on the whole. While they first entered into bargaining negotiations with Germany with misgivings and fears, there was general satisfaction with their outcome after the first two or three years of the experience. But gradually increasing pressure was applied, and soon the pressure became not merely economic, not merely a pressure for better terms of trade for Germany and for what were virtually forced loans, but for acceptance of a measure of German control over national policy in the various countries, including authority over direction of production in various Balkan countries away from manufactures and toward the provision of the foodstuffs and raw materials in most urgent demand within Germany.

A Hitlerian Europe would probably maintain a permanent residue of trade with noncontrolled areas. There would be a few items which it would be impossible or too costly to produce at home, whether in the same form or in a satisfactory substitute form, and which it would be too costly psychologically or otherwise to do without. But the terms on which Germany would accept such commodities from countries that were seriously dependent on the German controlled market would be terms involving not merely the rates at which the commodities should be paid for but also, wherever it seemed to serve German interests and ambitions, acceptance of German dictation of production plans and of German technical guidance and, no doubt, also of German political and military influence.

It should be noticed also that the larger the area under control, the smaller is the economic cost of self-sufficiency, the larger is the non-German population upon which German terms of trade can be imposed, and the greater is the scope for the authoritarian dictation of the production plan in dependent areas in the interests of the people in Germany proper. There is no basis in the logic of the case why a program of that sort should have any definite spatial limitations. There are obvious qualifications and obstacles—the inconveniences of distance, the limitations of administrative capacity —but the logic of the German program leaves no room for rigid boundaries and implies no specific point of satiety with respect to economic or political expansion.

Now, what is the significance for the United States of these developments? In the economic sphere the significance for us would not be as tragic as it would be say for an England left technically independent, but left an island having to trade on the German basis with a Hitler-controlled Europe plus important subsidiary areas outside Europe. For this country, both for natural reasons—its range of climates, the richness and variety of its natural resources, its great area and population—and because of the fact that for some hundred years we have in effect been training our economy to operate independently of the outside world, the shutting-off of the European market or the prevention of access to it except on German dictated and monopolistic terms would not be as tragic as it would be for England or, still more, for countries like Denmark or Switzerland. It would be important even for us. But we have already so fully exploited the possibilities of doing damage to our economy by the erection of trade barriers that the remaining possible damage which could be inflicted upon us is probably not as great as that we have already inflicted upon ourselves. Nevertheless, that remainder is still substantial and significant and would be particularly irksome in the short run until we had found ways of making adjustments to the new situation.

The closing to our trade of the Continental European market would mean a drastic reduction of American export trade and also a drastic reduction, if not total elimination, of the value to the American people of their substantial European investments. Incidentally, it would probably also mean a loss of value of the American-owned gold. It would also have other consequences, not of a strictly economic character, but which it would be absurdly pedantic to leave without mention merely for that reason.

The tremendous economic bargaining power which the German-controlled area has and will have, and especially the bargaining power it will have if the dictators can come to an agreement among themselves to operate in common against nontotalitarian countries, can be used to establish political and strategic footholds in areas important to us in a military sense. Also, it can be used to promote an ideological offensive against us. In so far also as the German commercial policy may add to the intensity of our apparently perpetual depression and may increase the degree in which our labor remains unemployed, it will promote internal tensions here—tensions which would be all the greater and the more menacing if, as is quite conceivable, German-controlled Europe gave a contrasting picture of an apparently skilfully managed, well-directed, smoothly working economy, with a rising standard of living—at least for Germans—with freedom from social discussion and debate and from party conventions, and with no visible or audible internal discontent.

Reinforced by the additional prestige of unparalleled military success, the German philosophy will tend to penetrate here. There will result two kinds of appeasement campaigns in this country— the one joyous and the other mournful. Some will be happily and readily, others will be sadly and in a defeatist mood, willing to come to terms with Hitler even if they be wholly his terms. There will not be any difference of consequence between the objective behavior of the two groups, and both groups will be sizable. One of them is already so.

What can be done about it? I would say that at this late date not much as far as the economic sphere is concerned, and that little of doubtful efficacy. In other spheres of action also, I fear, not much, and that even of more doubtful efficacy. I think we are probably going to embark on one defensive venture—I hope we are, and I wish it success—that is the attempt to develop some means of economic co-operation with noncontrolled areas for defensive purposes. That proposal has been presented in large part in terms of the Western Hemisphere. I have felt, myself, that this stress on the Western Hemisphere may be a mistake; that we ought not to undertake too rigid geographical commitments. We know that we must assume military responsibilities with respect to the Caribbean area and that assumption of responsibility for meeting the economic needs of that area is not beyond our capacity. The Caribbean area, moreover, can be given elastic boundaries, as circumstances and national interest dictate. "Western Hemisphere," on the other hand, is geographically a definite and inflexible term, and it embraces a southern area whose willingness to co-operate with us politically cannot be taken for granted, whose economic needs we can provide for, if at all, only at tremendous cost, and whose military security we can probably not guarantee except at tremendous risk to ourselves. The southern half of South America and our own country are more than continents apart—and not only in matters of mere distance—and no good will come from refusing frankly to acknowledge this ugly fact.

Overstress of a Western Hemisphere program may lead, moreover, to neglect of opportunities for co-operation with political and economic areas outside of the Americas which are much closer to us in culture and ideology than the Latin-American countries and which present more favorable prospects for economic co-operation on a basis of mutuality of considerations. There seems to me to be a real danger that we may use "talk" about Western Hemisphere policy and Western Hemisphere conferences without real agendas and without real results as psychological compensation for our failure to formulate and to take concrete and reasonably adequate steps toward fulfilment of a rational and courageous policy toward the outside world as a whole. There is at least some ground for suspicion that since the state of world affairs became clearly critical we have made "Pan-Americanism" our national vehicle for daydreaming, wishful thinking, and postponement of difficult and unpleasant but urgent decisions, corresponding to the appeasement policy of England and France before and after Munich.

There is, of course, something to be said on the other side. There are psychological values in saying "Western Hemisphere" even if what we really mean is the Caribbean area plus Canada. It may also be wise to conduct preliminary negotiations with all the Latin-American countries even if—and perhaps especially if—we do not think it likely that all of them could be persuaded to co-operate with us. Since special interest in the political integrity of *all* the American republics is a traditional American policy, it might be easier to win American approval for a financially expensive program if it could be presented as a fulfilment of the Monroe Doctrine. The smaller Latin-American republics might perhaps feel safer from encroachment on our part if their larger brothers were also participants in any compact with us.

Perhaps there are also strong military reasons why all the South American countries should be brought into any arrangement for common defensive action. It may be that the mere fact that there is on the map no complete water barrier between us and any American country makes it strategically important that the whole hemisphere be regarded as a unit for defense purposes. But to one layman at least it seems every day increasingly doubtful that a stretch of water is a more effective military barrier than an equal stretch of land which is roadless and consists largely of insurmountable mountain ranges and impassable jungle.

There is also the argument for a Western Hemisphere policy—probably the strongest one—that Latin America is to a substantial degree a cultural unity; that its political boundaries, and even its jungles and mountain ranges, are not effective barriers to the spread of ideas; and that we cannot expect to obtain adherence by one half of Latin America to a program of resistance to nazi and fascist programs and policies while the other half—whether by choice or from inability to resist economic or military pressure—comes to terms with the dictators.

A priori, the greater the number of countries which we can persuade to co-operate with us in a common program of political and economic resistance to the dictators, the greater will be the chances of our own successful resistance. The only real questions in my mind are, first, whether the southern Latin-American countries are willing to co-operate, and, second, whether an effective scheme can be worked out which would be acceptable both to them and to us. It is clear that we can induce these countries to enter into closer political relations with us and to stay out of the Hitlerian orbit if Hitler should have any desire of bringing them within it, only if we can make it possible for them to maintain a satisfactory economic existence outside that orbit and only if we can afford them sufficient military protection against being drawn within that orbit by force of arms. Their economic dependence upon Europe for export markets, their geographical isolation from us, and the existence within their boundaries of large German and Italian colonies presumably ready under proper circumstances to play the fifth-column role, these and other factors certainly provide justification for doubt both as to the military and as to the economic possibilities. For a year or two at least, while we are creeping toward military preparedness, we will be almost a negligible military factor, except with respect to the naval defense of our own and nearby coastlines. If England should soon be crushed, even this exception may no longer be valid. It is not at all obvious to the layman that, in any arrangement with the southern Latin-American countries involving military commitments on our part, we would be in any better position to carry them out than England was with respect to Poland or Norway. We will not be able, moreover, to keep out of Hitler's orbit any Latin-American area which tempts him merely by offering it naval defense, even unquestionably effective naval defense, against German aggression. We must also assure it of effective economic defense, of arrangements which will enable it to exist and to live on a standard of living not appreciably lower than that to which it has been accustomed or than may be offered to it by Hitler.

Our position with respect to the Caribbean area, Canada, and the various islands which lie off or near the coasts of this country, is substantially different. Their strategic importance to us is more obvious; their economic complementarity with us is much greater; we are more nearly in possession now of the military power to carry out any engagements we may make with them. But, I repeat, we will not be able to keep any area out of Hitler's orbit merely by offering it naval defense. We will also have to offer it the opportunity to maintain its economy on a satisfactory level.

As for our own ability, if necessary, to live apart from Europe and in a Western Hemisphere union, I think that if we are realistic in appraising the problems which today face us we will not regard this as one of the major ones. We have, for reasons of physical and human geography and under the influence of a hundred years of deliberate policy, adjusted ourselves already fairly substantially to living alone and liking it. With what is available to us from the Western Hemisphere—for that matter, with what is available to us from the Western Hemisphere north of the equator—the list of commodities which would not be available to us but which are urgently necessary is surprisingly small. There are many other commodities not now available in the Western Hemisphere which it would be exceedingly inconvenient for us to have to do without. The commodity experts, however, tell us that for most of them at least we could, if given time, find either usable substitutes or Western Hemisphere sources of supply adequate for the really urgent needs and could survive the period of adjustment without too much suffering through careful rationing of accumulated stocks.

There are only two commodities not available in the Western Hemisphere in anything like adequate quantities which are both of vital importance to American industry and American consumption standards and of great commercial importance in themselves—namely, rubber and tin. Even in these cases the question can be raised whether, given some years for adjustment and accumulated stocks and probable leakage even from a barricaded outside world to help tide over the adjustment period, the difficulties from enforced reliance on Western Hemisphere sources of supply would be unbearable. The progress in manufacture of synthetic substitutes for natural rubber has been very great in recent years—both as to quality and as to cost—and the physical possibilities of growth of natural rubber in the Western Hemisphere—its original home—also seem to be substantial. Bolivia produces a substantial quantity of tin, and some experts believe that it could provide us with all the tin urgently needed by us, since we use tin for many purposes which are either not of great importance or could be served fairly satisfactorily by other materials. If we were cut off from Straits Settlements tin our difficulty would be rather the absence of tin-smelting facilities than the absence of tin, and this lack is remediable and apparently is already in process of partial removal, although it is not clear that we yet know how satisfactorily to smelt Bolivian tin unmixed with other tin. It is to be noted, moreover, that our rubber and tin imports come mainly from British and Dutch Asiatic colonies and that Japan, rather than Hitler, or rather than Hitler directly, constitutes what menace there may be to the continuance of free economic intercourse with those areas.

Other important commodities can readily be thought of which are wholly or partially lacking in the Western Hemisphere, as, for instance, raw silk, jute, coarse wools, tea. Even total deprivation of these, however, would not involve disaster. I do not for a moment wish to minimize the importance of their contribution to our standard of living in normal times, but we must learn to distinguish in a crisis period between what are to be regarded as conveniences and what are genuine and urgent necessities. For the industrial uses of silk, rayon and synthetic fibers are becoming increasingly available and satisfactory. For the consumption-good users of silk—mostly the ladies—substitution of other fibers would not be a major adjustment once the unavailability of silk had brought about the inevitable changes in fashion. The major disturbance would fall rather on the silk-processing industries and their labor supply, and regional and occupational hardships would no doubt occur, but they would be temporary. In the case of coarse wools, such as are used mainly for carpet-making, our supplies also come mainly from outside the Western Hemisphere. It is cost rather than technical unsuitability, however, which shuts out the use of fine wools for carpeting. A wide range of nonwool substitutes are available, moreover, and the extent and manner of use of carpeting is probably more largely a matter of fashion than of inherent physical needs or convenience.

In the case of the uses of jute, it is again more a matter of cheapness than of inherent necessity which dictates the choice of jute in preference to other materials. The southern cotton growers would in fact welcome a prohibitive tariff on jute to promote the substitution of cotton for jute, and it has always seemed to them—wrongly, of course, under normal conditions—to be absurd to use jute bagging instead of cotton bagging for cotton baling, sugar bags, etc., when they were finding difficulty in marketing their cotton output.

There is a longer list of commodities, not important in their aggregate trade value but important as key products in industrial process, which are not available at all or in adequate quantities in the Western Hemisphere but which we cannot do without except at a very heavy cost. Industrial diamonds, tungsten, and antimony may be taken as representative examples of such commodities. Since, however, the danger which faces us with respect to our imports is not a total shutting-off of trade with non-American areas but subjection of such trade to terms dictated to us by Hitler and his European and Asiatic colleagues, probably the worst that could happen is that such commodities would become available to us only at very high unit prices. In the course of time and under the stimulus of these high prices domestic sources of supply, domestic substitutes, and new processes of production which could dispense with their use would be developed for many of them. In the interval, the incentive to the smuggler and the control evader would probably serve to moderate the impact of any deliberate restrictions of supply from controlled areas.

For the reasons given, therefore, I come to the conclusion that it will not be the burdens resulting from unavailability of vital commodities in the Western Hemisphere which would be the chief cost to us of our being cut off or of our cutting ourselves off from normal economic intercourse with the rest of the world. The difficult problem, I think, for both the United States and the rest of the Western Hemisphere, would be on the production side, in the adjustment of production to the disappearance of old markets and to the new channels of consumption rather than in the forced abstention from consumption because of the physical scarcity of hitherto imported goods. Unfortunately for effective Western Hemisphere economic co-operation, to a large extent Latin America does not have use for our export commodities, and to a much larger extent we either have no use or refuse to use and will continue to refuse to use its export commodities.

For the Western Hemisphere as a whole there are four great surpluses—wheat, cotton, coffee, and sugar. The Western Hemisphere would have to face the problem of diverting substantial quantities of productive resources from the production of these four commodities to other directions. In the case of at least three of these commodities and to a large extent of the fourth, because these are products of monoculture and products of regions which have specialized very intensively in the production of these single commodities, the problem of adjustment would be all the more serious.

For twenty leading export commodities of the Latin-American countries as a whole, the total exports in 1938 amounted to roughly one and a half billion dollars, of which four hundred and fifty million, roughly, went to the United States and over eleven hundred million went to non–Western Hemisphere countries. The United States in 1938 imported from other than Latin-American countries goods, which in the trade statistics are classified as the same goods, to the amount of approximately four hundred million dollars. It might seem that the United States could easily divert these purchases to Latin-American countries. But the matter is not so simple. In the first place, the commodities imported by the United States from non–Latin-American countries and the commodities exported by Latin America elsewhere than to the United States may be quite different and not substitutable for one another even though they carry the same name in the trade statistics. Second, included in these four hundred million dollars are at least fifty million dollars of imports for re-export to markets which are now largely under Hitler's control. Third, one hundred and fifty million dollars represent imports from the Philippines, which presumably must be permitted to continue. Fourth, some forty-five million dollars represent imports of tin, but the tin exported by Bolivia is unsmelted tin, whereas the tin imported into the United States is smelted tin. Until there are smelters in the Western Hemisphere these Bolivian exports are not a substitute for the American imports of tin. Another fifty million dollars, roughly, of these four hundred million dollars represent imports from West Indian colonies and from Canada and Newfoundland. This leaves only something like one hundred to one hundred and fifty million dollars of present American imports from non–Western Hemisphere sources of the commodities which are major exports of Latin America.

If we were to remove import duties on imports of these commodities from Latin America, we could probably absorb several hundred million dollars additional annually of these present exports of Latin America. But that would intensify our agricultural problem, and, as far as my observation goes, it is an elementary principle of American politics that no solution which is not acceptable to the American farmers is a practicable solution. We cannot expect therefore any substantial contribution to a solution of the problem from this direction.

Full recovery of prosperity in the United States would promote adjustment. These 1938 figures that I have used are not sacrosanct; they are a function of the state of American and world prosperity in that year. If American prosperity increased, our imports of Latin-American products would increase.

Allowing, however, for all these adjustments, there would still be a substantial residue, at least for a while, of Latin-American productive capacity that would be without markets if Latin America's economic ties with the outside world were cut off—a residue which, most conservatively estimated, would reach at least five hundred million dollars and would probably reach seven hundred and fifty million dollars a year. If we are seriously to consider entering into any form of economic union with the Western Hemisphere we will have to face the probability that we will be asked to contribute from five hundred to seven hundred and fifty million dollars a year—at least for a few years—not as an outright cash subsidy, but to finance their storing of goods which they are producing and which nobody wants or to finance the development of productive facilities for new types of goods which we do want. If we are not willing to donate our money or invest it or gamble with it—whichever is the most accurate term for the operation—along lines such as these, I feel sure that the scheme has no chance of acceptance.

If the union could be carried through, presumably one of its objectives would be to deal on a monopolistic basis with an outside agency that is also bargaining with it on a monopolistic basis, and, if bargaining is found impossible with the outside area or if the terms that are offered are not acceptable, at least to find some way of getting along without trade relations with the outside area by extending the degree of complementarity between Latin America and ourselves. I suppose also that the agreement would have political clauses and that we would ask for assurances as to air bases and possibly naval stations and assurances as to co-operation in defense against political penetration by the totalitarian countries.

I do not think an arrangement of this sort can be or need be justified on strictly economic grounds. In a normal, peaceful world the strong probabilities are that the costs of administering such a plan— and especially the costs to the principal partner in the undertaking—would be greater than any possible gains from the exploitation of even unilateral, monopoly bargaining power. No one, however, is proposing the plan as an ideal long-run program. It has been devised and is being promoted strictly as an expedient to tide over an emergency, in the hope that it will enable Latin America and ourselves, acting in combination, to bargain on reasonable terms, and without subjection to political demands, with a monopolistically bargaining outside area or, failing this, to live within ourselves without unbearable injury to our standard of living. In the background also is clearly the hope that protection of Latin America against economic pressure from the dictators will increase both its chances and our own of preserving our own modes of social life against the nazi-fascist menace.

Whether or not the dangers facing us are sufficiently real and sufficiently imminent to justify our embarking on this uncertain enterprise depends, it seems to me, primarily on the fate of the British fleet. If England survives as a naval power, a better plan for dealing with both Hitler's trade methods and his military power would, I believe, be available than the Western Hemisphere policy. Close co-operation with the British Empire and with any other surviving and willing democracies for purposes of economic, political, and military defense, as a temporary policy without constitutional features and without regional restrictions as such, would provide, I believe, greater security at less expense, with a more balanced allocation of the expense and with greater promise of durability while the emergency lasts than would any conceivable project of Western Hemisphere union. But this is counting on the survival of England and of England's naval power, which it is no longer safe for us to do.

The Western Hemisphere program, therefore, cannot properly be appraised as if it purported to be an ideal program for a well-ordered world. It is rather an expedient—a meager and possibly ineffective one—for dealing with an emergency situation in which we have surrendered or had taken from us or are psychologically inhibited from using other conceivable expedients. The only real alternative still remaining is alliance with England, and it seems clear that the country will not be willing to regard this as an acceptable one until after it has ceased to be available. We had better win the co-operation of the Latin-Americans if we can, even if the price in dollars should seem high. It would be well for us to remember that we rather than they are the suitors, that they are appraising our possible contribution both of economic aid and of effective military protection more modestly— and perhaps more realistically—than we are, and that, except for dollars, whose military and even economic value we are prone to overestimate, we really have little to offer them in return for the risks they take in aligning themselves with us. I believe, moreover, that we should not insist upon an all-or-none participation; that we should choose real co-operation by some in preference to merely formal verbal commitments by all; and especially that we should not let hostility to our proposals by the southern republics, if it should make its appearance, deter us from coming, if we can, to a real agreement with the northern ones.

# THE ROLE OF SHIPPING IN THE WORLD ORDER

*By* CHARLES C. COLBY
Professor of Geography

# THE ROLE OF SHIPPING IN THE WORLD ORDER

IN THE United States and especially in the Middle West overseas shipping has been regarded as a natural part of the world order. The average citizen takes for granted the regular export of goods to foreign countries and the presence in our markets of a great variety of moderately priced commodities gathered from all parts of the world. The essential and desirable foods and materials are expected to be abundant and cheap. Where they come from and how they get here does not matter. There is, moreover, but casual appreciation of the facts that this flow of commodities forms the center of interest in international relations and constitutes visible and concrete evidence of the present world order. Nor is the vital role played by shipping in maintaining this world order well understood. Let the shipowner and the shipbroker worry about shipping; the general public has more important things to think about. The multiplicity of events of the World War, the postwar boom, the depression, and the present conflict, however, have shown and are showing that the economical employment of shipping is of vital concern to all of us—to our comfort, to our pocket-books, and even to our existence as a free people.

### TYPES OF SHIPPING

The overseas-carrying trade of the world is divided between tramp or charter vessels prepared to trade on short notice wherever cargoes can be found and liner vessels with scheduled sailings on defined routes. The tramp is a single vessel operated as a unit; the line is a group of vessels or, more correctly, a volume of tonnage operated as a unit.

Tramp vessels are economically operated when they carry full cargoes of a single commodity. As this means from about 2,000 to 8,000 long tons of the commodity, the tramp can be used in transporting only those relatively few commodities which move in huge quantities from definite ports and at particular times.

Coal, iron ore, wheat, sugar, lumber, and petroleum rank high in the list of charter commodities. In many cases the movement of such commodities is highly seasonal. The traffic is huge during one part of the year and dwindles to nothing in the other seasons. Argentina, for example, needs a hundred ships or more a month from November to March to move its wheat and maize to Europe. During these same months and in these same bottoms most of the seven or eight millions of tons of

British coal which coalless Argentina needs are imported. In the remainder of the year the Argentine ports see relatively few tramp vessels. The vessels, however, find employment in other ports of the world. This mobility of tramp vessels is evidence of the flexibility of sea transport and lies back of the low cost of many commodities in world markets.

Liner vessels may be passenger vessels, cargo vessels, or a combination of both. Some lines, like Cunard, emphasize passenger service; others, like the Furness-Withy Company, are mainly freight carriers. In most cases liner vessels are of larger size and greater speed than tramp vessels. On many routes they are economically operated when they carry a combination of passengers, freight, mail, and express. Thus, anything which adds to or takes away any part of one of these types of traffic directly affects the company's revenues and, indirectly, the number and type of sailings it can offer. If, for example, the airplane of the future takes mail and passengers from the liner vessels on a particular route, the steamship services might need to be curtailed or be supported by government subsidies. It may be that the airplane will do more harm than good in overseas transport.

The great service of the liner vessel is regularity of operation. It makes possible a regular flow of commodities in large or small quantities throughout the year. Liner companies tend to stabilize conditions on a particular route and always are interested in further stabilization. To this end the management of a line commonly joins with the other lines in its territory in agreements as to rates, services, and schedules. The agreements are reached through conferences. These conferences are regional leagues of shipping companies and to a high degree they establish the world order in so far as shipping is concerned.

The number of steamship conferences has varied from time to time, but in a recent year twenty-eight were reported. Notable examples are the Far East Conference, the Australian Conference, the Caribbean Conference, and the North Atlantic Conference.[1] Before the World War the conferences were limited to the European nations engaged in shipping, with British and German influence predominating. Since then Japanese and United States and other lines have participated in some of the conferences.

The World War and the international conditions which followed it accelerated forces already under way in ocean transportation. An important ex-

---

[1] The original pool between the continental steamship companies was formed in 1892 and included the Hamburg-Amerika Line, the North German Lloyd, the Red Star Line (Antwerp), and the Holland-American Line (Rotterdam). This pool was widely known as the N.D.L.V. (Nordatlantisher Dampfer Linien Verband). Its major interest was the emigrant traffic from Europe to the United States.

ample is the increasing emphasis on liner traffic as compared with tramp traffic. In 1913–14 out of every hundred steel vessels suitable for ocean trade fifty-eight were owned by corporations operating lines of steamers and forty-two were general traders or tramps. By 1925 the proportion had become seventy-three liners to twenty-seven tramps.[2] This change had an important bearing on the regulation of ocean-free rates. In the past the tramp vessel competed with liner vessels in many trades, especially in carrying bulk and seasonal cargoes. This competition helped to regulate marine rates.[3] With the decline of the tramp this influence has been lessened and the rates are increasingly made in the regional conferences of liner companies. This situation tends to further the consolidation of shipping facilities and to place the financial control of such facilities in the hands of a relatively few organizations. The World War also increased the amount of government ownership and control of shipping and to a degree again reduced the importance of individual enterprise. At the current outlook (June, 1940) the present war may still further

[2] E. T. Chamberlain, "Liner Predominance in Transoceanic Shipping," *Bureau of Foreign and Domestic Commerce, Trade Information Bulletin No. 448*, p. 2.

[3] J. Russell Smith, *Influence of the Great War upon Shipping* ("Preliminary Economic Studies of the War," No. 9 [New York: Carnegie Endowment for International Peace, 1919]), pp. 20–21.

restrict the operation of ships by private individuals. The tendency is away from rather than toward the freedom of the seas.

## TYPES OF COMMODITIES CARRIED BY
### SHIPPING

In a normal year the world's sea-borne trade, as represented by imports into all countries, probably ranges from 250,000,000 to 300,000,000 long tons each year.[4] Although this estimate includes most if not all the commodities known to commerce, the major part of it arises in connection with the demand for food and for raw materials for construction and manufacture. Lumber and wood products, textile materials, wheat, coal, petroleum, the ores—iron, copper, lead, zinc, and tin—all fill many ships. The list of commodities is too long for ready generalization but from the shipping standpoint commodities may be classified in three groups, namely: (1) rough, low-priced commodities, such as coal, timber, and the like; (2) bulky commodities of medium value, such as grain, textile materials, crude metals, hides and skins, and the more bulky manufactures; (3) fine goods of all kinds which are of high value in relation to their

---

[4] For statistical material in regard to shipping and trade in the years immediately preceding the World War the author is indebted to the *Reports of the Departmental Committee Appointed by the Board of Trade To Consider the Position of the Shipping and Shipbuilding Industries after the War* (London, 1918).

bulk. The first group—namely, rough, low-priced commodities—is associated with tramp shipping. The second group moves partly in tramps and partly in liner vessels, whereas the third group, the fine goods of all kinds, moves wholly in liner ships. These groups of commodities contain both the necessities and the luxuries of our daily life. Whatever affects them affects us. If they are abundant and cheap in the international areas of major concern, the plane of living tends to rise; if they are scarce and costly, the world's standard of living, speaking broadly, tends to decline. During the century ending in 1914, commodities increased in variety and abundance, their price declined, their use increased greatly, and in many areas the plane of living improved. Much of the credit for this abundance goes to the development of shipping and railway transportation which featured the latter part of the nineteenth century.

### AREAS AND ROUTES OF MAJOR CONCERN
### TO SHIPPING

The commercial world, that is, the parts of the world equipped with the facilities and agencies of trade, covers much but not all of the land surface of the world. There are, however, large areas with little or no trade. Such areas lie beyond the dimensions of the commercial world as defined here. Within the commercial world seven areas are of major significance to shipping and, in fact, to practically every aspect of the international scene. These all-important areas are (1) Western Europe, (2) the eastern half of the United States, (3) the middle-latitude countries of South America, (4) India, (5) the East Indian region, (6) Japan and Eastern China, and (7) Australasia.

To serve the commercial regions of the world there are about 30,000 merchant ships, but not more than 8,000 are used in overseas business. On one summer's date in 1938 Britain alone had 9,292 merchant ships, big and little, actually in service. Those who attended the New York exposition will remember the huge map showing the distribution of British vessels on that day. The map showed many British ships in the waters of the major commercial regions, but the greatest concentration was in the North Sea and nearby waters and included many small vessels. On the high seas the North Atlantic route stood out, for it is the great shipping lane between Eastern United States and Western Europe. British ships on that day also were numerous on the long route which leads from Britain and the other countries of Western Europe via Gibraltar and Suez to India and beyond. Because this route in its course to the Far East serves many populous countries, it is the prime route in terms of ports of call.

# THE ROLE OF SHIPPING

Shipping is world wide in its field of operation but highly localized in its ownership. All but two of the twelve flags of importance in the maritime world are flags of European countries. Except for the shipping of the United States and Japan, most of the ships of the world are of European origin and are under European control. In June, 1914, the merchant marine of the United Kingdom comprised 45 per cent of the world's steam tonnage (11,500,000 tons out of about 26,000,000 tons net). Since then, the relative position of the United Kingdom has declined to about 30 per cent of the world's total, but it still has the largest, the most up-to-date, and probably the most efficient merchant marine in the world. Before the World War Germany held second place with 12 per cent of the world's shipping. Since the war, however, the United States, with 15 per cent of the total, has held second place, with six other countries—namely, Norway, Japan, Germany, France, Italy, and the Netherlands—closely contending for third place.[5]

In terms of world order the rank of the nations in shipping is less important than the extraordinary dominance of Western Europe. This area, long the active heart of the commercial world, has built and operated most of the world's ships. In these ships

[5] Lloyd's *Register*.

goods from all parts of the world have moved to Western Europe, and from Western Europe other goods have moved to all parts of the world. Farmers, miners, lumbermen, and others in all regions have looked to Western Europe as a market area. For more than a century this has been part of the world order. The World War profoundly disrupted this order. It brought, for example, a sense of insecurity to nations dependent upon foreign flags for the movement of their overseas trade. Out of the disruption the United States and Japan came forward as maritime nations. The present conflict threatens to disrupt the world order even more profoundly.

Thus far we have been concerned with the technique, the facts, and the areas of world shipping. It remains to examine another vital phase of the matter, namely, the question of the policy under which shipping has operated. As Britain has controlled nearly half the world's shipping, its policy in large measure has set the pace—has established the rules of the game. An examination of Britain's policy, therefore, should bring us as near an understanding of shipping in the world order as can be obtained in the brief span of a lecture hour.

### BRITAIN'S MARITIME POLICY

Because of the multiplicity of events since the World War the most satisfactory time to examine

Britain's position in world trade and shipping is in the years immediately preceding the war. The British Committee on Shipping, reporting in 1918, estimated that in 1912 more than 50 per cent of the world's sea-borne trade, as represented by the value of the imports into all countries, had one or both terminals within the British Empire and that the trade where one terminal was in the United Kingdom amounted to about 40 per cent of the total. As has been stated, 45 per cent of the world's shipping at that time was under the flag of the United Kingdom. In the twenty years preceding 1914 there were built in the world 25,000,000 tons of steam shipping; two-thirds of this great volume were built in the United Kingdom. In 1912 British shipping carried 52 per cent of the total sea-borne trade of the world. It carried 90 per cent of the trade within the Empire, 60 per cent of the trade between the Empire and foreign countries, and 30 per cent of the trade between foreign countries.

The commanding position held by the United Kingdom in the trade by sea was the result of slow but persistent growth over four or five centuries. The growth began about the close of the sixteenth century. At that time England was counted a poor country with scarcely 4,000,000 inhabitants. Even in 1700 wool was still England's largest export. As late as the reign of Elizabeth, England imported all "artificiality," as finished manufactures were called. It was from these meager circumstances that Britain developed supremacy in the carrying trade. The development came in three fairly definite stages.

The first period in the evolution of Britain as a maritime nation was from the close of the sixteenth century to the time of the Industrial Revolution. This period was marked by a series of exhausting wars on the Continent in which Britain became the foremost power in Europe. The mercantile policy during this period was the development of industry and the creation of a strong self-sufficing state. To this end was subordinated certain English interests which conflicted with this policy, and the interests of the Colonies were subordinated to this policy. The famous Navigation Laws were the maritime expression of this policy. The main provisions of these laws were (1) foreign vessels were excluded from the inter-Empire and coasting trades and (2) foreign vessels were prohibited from importing into Britain or any of its possessions any goods unless (*a*) they were the product of the country in which the vessel belonged and (*b*) they were imported in such vessels directly from the country of origin.[6]

[6] *Parliamentary Return*, No. 338 (London, 1902). This contains a "Reprint of the Appendix to the Fifth Report of the Select Committee on the Navigation Laws, 1847."

The Navigation Laws apparently were aimed primarily at Holland's entrepôt trade. They drove Dutch shipping into the North Sea and Baltic trade where British ships had been active. This brought distress to and protests from an important sector of British shipping. The laws, however, helped to drive British ships out to sea and thus laid the basis for the remarkable developments during the next stage in Britain's maritime evolution.

The second period in the evolution of Britain as a maritime power covers the Industrial Revolution and the Napoleonic Wars. For convenience of statement let the period extend from 1750 to 1850. During this period industrial discoveries and inventions, and especially the use of steam power, gradually revolutionized the economy of the United Kingdom and modified its mercantile policy. In this connection it should be remembered that abundant supplies of coal and iron near the seacoast enabled the United Kingdom to reap the benefits of the new discoveries and to remain for a long time the most important if not the only manufacturing country of importance in the world. During this period the population increased rapidly and the country grew wealthy and became increasingly dependent on the outside world not only for food and raw materials but for a market for its manufactured goods. As a result the Navigation Laws were gradually relaxed, being finally repealed in 1849. Interestingly enough the first relaxations were in favor of the United States, then Britain's principal competitor in shipping. Great forces were at work, however, and the subsequent differentiation of the economic interests of the United Kingdom and the United States already was discernible.

The third period in Britain's evolution saw the increase of the British Merchant Marine from the 4,000,000 tons of 1850 to the 11,500,000 tons of 1914. During the same interval the overseas shipping of the United States declined to less than a million tons. Britain's modern position in maritime affairs dates from the substitution of steam for sailing power and of iron and steel for wood. It represents an industrial and commercial economy developed on the best located island area in the world. During the same time the energies of the United States became absorbed in the settlement and development of its western territories. It became continental in outlook in harmony with the fact that our riches of land and minerals lie inland. The development of the two countries was harmonious, however, for the economy of the one buttressed and supplemented the other. To a marked degree they epitomized the world order of the time.

During the period of 1850 to 1914 Britain developed a policy of equal treatment of all flags in all areas. Foreign flags were given equality of treatment with British vessels in British ports, and the British aimed at securing similar treatment for British shipping in foreign ports. This was the period of "free trade" and it was characterized by a vast increase in world trade and a rising standard of living in many countries. The United States prospered under it, and during this period Germany enjoyed a prosperity and a freedom of thought and action which it had not known before and which it may not know again.

The position of the United Kingdom in world affairs at the outbreak of the World War was based on a closely related structure of industry, trade, and shipping. This structure in its full complexity eludes brief characterization. On the maritime side, however, certain elements stand out conspicuously. The British led in shipbuilding. They were the first to apply the discoveries of the Industrial Revolution to ocean transport, they developed the world's largest merchant fleet, and they kept their fleet up to date by a policy of selling their old ships to other countries and by building new vessels to replace the old ones. They had large supplies of good coal at the seaboard, and they exported large tonnages of this coal to other countries and to the fuel stations along the ocean lanes. This export coal moved at low rates because the ships which brought the great imports of foodstuffs and raw materials preferred to lift coal at low rates on their outward voyages rather than to carry fruitless ballast. This inward and outward balance of heavy traffic was the basis of Britain's leadership in the tramp traffic of the world. Most of the fuel stations along the sea lanes were owned and operated by British companies. In large measure they sold to British liners coal brought by British tramps from British mines. They of course sold coal at the same price to vessels of any and all flags, for the plan of equal treatment of all flags in all areas was the essence of British maritime policy.

As Britain imported and exported large quantities of goods not suited to tramp vessels, there existed a natural basis for leadership in liner traffic. Regular sailings to any or all parts of the commercial world have been more characteristic of Britain than of any other country. This facilitates the movement of passengers, express, mail, and freight and is a great asset in supplying customers in all parts of the world. World-wide banking services and commercial agencies implemented and encouraged the development of all this trade. It is this world-wide structure which is being challenged at the present moment.

### GERMANY'S MARITIME POLICY

Germany's maritime policy has called for more highly centralized control of its merchant fleet than that of any other country.  This was true before the World War and it has held since then.  In 1913, for example, over 60 per cent of Germany's shipping was controlled by the "Reederei-Vereinigung"—a group of ten lines which was to all extent and purposes a German mercantile shipping union trading in most parts of the world.  The character of this union is shown by the fact that a contract with one of these lines was a contract with all the others.  The German fleet was distinctly a liner fleet.  In fact, the Germans have never shown much active interest in the type of individual initiative required in the operation of tramp vessels.  Because of the highly centralized control which has prevailed in German shipping, the German companies have exercised great influence in the steamship conferences.  In some cases this influence apparently has been all out of proportion to the amount of shipping employed in the area in question.

German foreign trade developed rapidly in the three decades preceding the World War.  A large part of this trade was with countries on the land frontier, but there also was a great expansion in overseas trade.  In 1913, 50 per cent of the imports by weight came from countries on the land frontier and 83 per cent of the exports went to those countries.  This emphasis on land trade was in harmony with the central position of Germany in the continent of Europe and is a factor which should not be underestimated in judging the direction of emphasis in Germany's efforts in the future.

Germany's imports by sea in 1913 were not much less than the volume of imports into the United Kingdom, and like Britain's imports they came from nearly all parts of the commercial world. The volume of exports by sea, however, was only a fourth of that of Britain. Germany had no sea export equivalent in bulk to Britain's exports of coal. Germany's coal exports were large but they crossed the land frontier. In terms of value, the sea-borne trade of Germany and the German overseas possessions were about a third that of the British Empire. This trade, however, was of sufficient size to justify the employment of a considerable amount of merchant shipping.

Although in the decade preceding the World War German merchant vessels operated in most parts of the world, the major emphasis in German shipping was in the North Atlantic. Emigration from Europe to North America provided most of the profits in this trade and was the subject of acute controversy in the North Atlantic Conference. After southeastern Europe became the area of origin of the majority of emigrants, Germany's central position in Europe made it possible for her to control much of this emigration. The competition of the British and German lines over this all-important traffic was especially severe after 1910. In fact, the agreement under which they divided trade came to an end at the close of 1913. Although negotiations were still nominally under way up to the declaration of war, practically, they had fallen through.

The World War witnessed Germany's great challenge to Britain's control of shipping and thus to the world order of that time. The submarine was the instrument of attack, but the scarcity of shipping occasioned by the bottling-up of the German marine and by the large amounts of shipping requisitioned for the war purposes of the allies furnished the opportunity.[7]

During the first two years of the war the submarine was in the experimental stage, and although many vessels were sunk they were mainly small craft in the North Sea and had little or no effect on the inflow of foods and materials into Britain and France. In February, 1917, the submarine advanced into the ocean and began to sink big ships—each one a substantial part of world shipping. In this connection it should be recognized that for many decades the average size of ocean-going vessels has steadily increased.[7] The

[7] At the end of 1913 the merchant fleet of the United Kingdom included 8,855 steam vessels of less than 1,000 tons net and 3,747 vessels of and above 1,000 tons net. The tonnage of the former group amounted to only 1,100,000 tons net, whereas the latter group included 10,173,000 net tons. The early submarine attack was on the smaller vessels and had no serious effect.

efficient ship is a large ship. Britain, in fact, carried on its overseas services with less than four thousand ships. This is the strength of the British fleet in peace times and its weakness in time of war. From January to August 1, 1917, losses were six hundred larger vessels. After February the losses averaged eighty large vessels per month. By September 1, 1917, Germany had destroyed about 5,000,000 tons net or 20 per cent of the world's shipping.

The submarine attack brought the United States into the conflict. An important part of our participation was the building of ships in the American manner, namely, by building identical parts and assembling them into identical ships. Up to this time ships had been built as individual units and several months were required to build even a small vessel. Germany, therefore, was confident that the United States could not build ships fast enough to have any bearing on the conflict. They were certain we could not fabricate ships as we do automobiles. Interestingly enough, no one in this country, thoroughly schooled in the assembly line, ever doubted we could fabricate ships. Perhaps we were too ignorant of the difficulties of building ships to know what we were up against. Many mistakes were made, but finally models that would work were designed, and week by week ships spilled into the sea at a rate that the losses from the submarine could not possibly match. In betting against the fabrication of ships in the United States, Germany wagered against the essential genius of the American people in manufacture, and betting against the genius of a people is never safe.

Following the World War Germany's foreign trade recovered slowly. By 1936, however, it amounted in value to roughly three-fifths what it was in 1913. The point of real significance is that again the major flow of trade was across the land frontiers. Geographically and economically this is as logical as is our large trade with Canada. It is the natural sphere of action for the major part of Germany's trade. By 1929 Germany had regained its customary rank in world trade with approximately 10 per cent of the total. As a nation it was exceeded only by the United States and the United Kingdom.

## SHIPPING IN THE FUTURE

The future of overseas shipping is none too clear. The circumstances and policies of recent years make predictions hazardous. It can be argued, however, that without overseas trade and shipping, the people of many sections of the world will have to do without many commodities to which they have become accustomed. It is incredible that, having developed world trade and tasted its benefits, the nations of the world should retard and restrict it as they have done since the World War. Britain's experience since the World War illustrates the trend. Following the war the British made great efforts to continue their policy of equal treatment of all flags in all parts of the world. The tide of events was against them. Tariffs, duties, and other restrictions to trade were raised in country after country. Nationalism swept in. Eventually, Britain abandoned its time-honored policy of free trade, and overseas trade declined. The Ottawa and London conferences represented attempts at realignment of trade to emphasize trade within the Empire. Then into the international scene came new ideas of government in Europe and new implements of transport—the airplane and the tank. In Canada these new implements opened up new sections and showed what they can do in times of peace. In Europe they introduced the modern inferno and threatened the whole structure of the world order.

If Britain wins the war the future of world shipping can be foreseen. As soon as possible (if the time ever arrives) a return to the policy of equal treatment of all flags in all parts of the world can be expected. The world can look forward to reasonable efficiency in ship operation and to a world order in which shipping will be regarded as a business to be utilized for the development of international trade. Many countries again will profit from the essential genius of Britain in operating ships and in developing trade.

If Germany wins, no prophecy can be made. The policy is likely to be against the logic of geography and the rational evolution of world economy. The variables overwhelm the equation.

If Germany attempts to carry its aggressive program overseas, where will it strike? Before 1914 German shipping was the spearhead of German aggression. It was used effectively in furthering the national objectives especially in the Near East and Middle East, in Equatorial Africa, in South America and Caribbean America, and in the Far East. German competition at that time was formidable through a combination of factors: (1) overproduction at home, (2) the care of the manufacturer to meet the precise demand of the overseas customer, (3) the organization of trades and transport, and (4) the co-ordination of these factors under able political direction. Will these be the areas and the techniques of emphasis in the future? Will the maritime policy of Germany and the manner of their implementation be such as to provide the world's sea lanes with low-cost shipping services? Will overseas trade be stimulated or restricted? These are matters of profound significance in the world of the future.

There is another and geographically more logical possibility for German emphasis in the future.

It will be remembered that the larger part of Germany's foreign trade has been across her land frontiers. Perhaps Germany will endeavor to consolidate her position on the Continent. Will she attempt to control the vast area between the North and Baltic seas on the one hand and the Black Sea on the other?[8] Is a revival of the Berlin to Bagdad emphasis to be expected? An extension along this route would give control of abundant supplies of oil, the lack of which was an important factor in Germany's defeat in the World War and is a major threat at present. The axis could be controlled from the air, for the experience of years of flying shows that the flying conditions along this route are favorable through much of the year. Having developed the airplane as an instrument of war, is it not likely that Germany will attempt to use it in times of peace? To the extent which passengers, mail, express, and light freight are diverted from shipping on the Mediterranean-Asiatic sea route, the profit of operating ships on that route probably will decline. The competition of air and sea transport probably was coming in any case, but as a result of the present war it may be hastened and perhaps perverted in unexpected ways. If Germany does attempt to build a land empire somewhat along the lines suggested, both time and ef-

[8] "Toward a 'Mittel-Europa,'" *Barrons' Financial Weekly* (New York), August 24, 1936, pp. 13-18.

fort will be required. Something of the same forces which turned the eyes of the United States inland from the sea in the last century probably will be at work again.

In this brief review of the role of shipping in the world order but little has been said about the United States. This may appear unfortunate in view of the fact that for many years the United States has been the second country in world trade. Actually, however, the United States has been content to have its exports and imports largely move in the ships of Britain and other nations. This country prospered under that regime. The World War, however, cut off many areas from their accustomed trade with Western Europe. These areas turned to the United States and Japan for the goods and services which they could not obtain from Europe. Some, but by no means all, of this trade reverted to Europe after the war. In addition, both the United States and Japan have developed other trade.

In the fifty years preceding 1914, the United States had not been actively interested in overseas shipping. It had built an adequate steel navy and had established certain lines of contract mail vessels, more especially in an attempt to improve its position in the Pacific following the annexation of

Hawaii and the acquisition of the Philippine Islands.[9]

At the outbreak of the World War the entire overseas fleet of vessels of 12 knots or over under the United States flag was confined to eight companies. By 1925, however, the American overseas liner tonnage had increased from 820,000 to 8,738,000 gross tons. This was over three-fourths of the world's increase of liner tonnage during this period.

The United States, with about 15 per cent of total sea tonnage, possesses the second largest merchant marine in the world. This country, therefore, occupies the relative position occupied by Germany before the World War. The United States now has ships on many lanes, and in working the world's shipping lanes its vessels have the fundamental advantage of the United States being the only major nation facing both the Atlantic and the Pacific oceans. Since the opening of the Panama Canal, American companies have capitalized that advantage by operating ships around the world. In this service American vessels have taken full advantage of the nation's long-established policy of restricting intercoastal trade to vessels under the American flag. Thus the ships of the United States can carry goods on the long haul from New York to

[9] Chamberlain, *op. cit.*, p. 28.

San Francisco and other west-coast ports, whereas other vessels cannot. If the United States comes to play a larger part in world trade, perhaps such restrictive policies may need to be abandoned.

That the United States will have an active interest in overseas shipping is almost certain in view of its interocean position, its land and other natural resources, its highly productive industries, and the intelligent energy of its people. These are long-run considerations, whereas the immediate effects of the World War and the present conflict are short-run considerations. The national and international policies which may grow out of this war, however, are likely to be long run in their effect. Let us hope that a rational policy for the United States and the world may be forthcoming. Let us hope that shipping may continue to play the effective and efficient role in the world order that it has in the past. The principles underlying this policy have been made clear by a century of experience. We know that whatever nation or nations may take the lead in world shipping, the wisest and sanest policy yet developed is that of equal treatment of all flags in all parts of the world. This policy is in harmony with the fundamental pattern of world geography and with the general welfare of mankind.

# INTERNATIONAL LAW AND THE
# WORLD ORDER

*By* QUINCY WRIGHT
Professor of International Law

# INTERNATIONAL LAW AND THE
# WORLD ORDER

SOME of you may have gained the impression that these lectures are being given for the benefit of the technologically unemployed, such as the free traders and the international lawyers. Why talk of international law in times like these? Our only answer is the long view to which Professor Schevill, with the freedom from the present which is the happy lot of historians, invited us. To consider international law in these times of transition we must accept this advice and get a perspective. We must see international law not as an aggregate of isolated rules but as the system of assumptions and logical deductions that characterize our civilization. It is true a system of law is something more than a logical system. It is a logical system in operation, continually buffeted by the pressure of events. "The life of the law," said Justice Holmes, "is not logic but experience."[1] Experience, with events and conditions, opinions and policies, continually distorts the logic of law never more than it is doing with international law at present. Every legal system anticipates some

[1] O. W. Holmes, *The Common Law* (Boston: Little Brown & Co., 1881), chap. 1.

violations of its rules and principles, in this respect differing from a scientific system. But it can normally deal with such violations by the processes of repression and accommodation. Events, however, may so shatter existing assumptions that the whole structure becomes unreal and ceases to be important, thus marking the end of a society or of a civilization.

International law is the body of mutually consistent rules, principles, and standards observed in the practice, professions, and protests of the members of the family of nations. Its basic assumptions have been the independence of each national state qualified by the duty of each to respect the domain, the status, the nationals, and the jurisdiction of the others and to observe the treaties to which it is a party. Has nonobservance of these assumptions become so general and habitual as to mark a turn in history? Is international law today suffering fatal blows from the course of events such as were suffered by Roman law in the fifth century and by medieval law in the fifteenth century? Before answering, let us consider the function of law and the extent to which international law has served this function in the past.

A system of law provides the standards and institutions uniting a political society, the rules and principles for settling the disputes of its members when they are unable to reach agreement, and the procedures and agencies for maintaining order and justice within the society. *Ubi societas ibi jus est.* Jurists have recognized that society and law are two sides of the same shield. Wherever one exists there also the other will be found.

International lawyers have faced this proposition with some embarrassment. They have recognized the difficulty of giving the name "society" to the group of frequently warring states claiming unlimited sovereignty and ready to transcend all rules —customary or conventional—when immediate political interest seems to require. Yet if there is not a society of nations, can there be a law of nations?

Most jurists have answered that there is a society of nations, although a primitive one. They have cited the common background of Christian and of classic civilization among the states which originally constituted that society; the common ideals of humanism, liberalism, tolerance, and scientific method which inspired the Renaissance thinkers who first conceived the idea of a secular society of independent states; the gradual growth of that society through the expansion of its ideas, its system of government, its technology, and its law throughout the world, followed by the formal recognition and admission to the original family of nations of the new states of America and the old states of Asia and Africa; the development of communication, trade, and cultural exchange weaving these states together into an interdependent whole, especially during the nineteenth century; and, finally, the elaboration of numerous international institutions to regulate and administer in the common interest the new relations developing from this interdependence and from the progress of science and invention.

Such a résumé creates an impressive picture of a growing world community whose development, while interrupted, has not been stopped by depressions, revolutions, or wars. Jurists with this picture before them have labored to assist this development by improving the institutions and procedures of world government, and by developing international law so that it will constitute a more perfect frame for the emerging federal world, more adequate rules for settling disputes among states, and more certain procedures for maintaining order and justice within the society. To such jurists the sovereignty of the nations of the world has been no different in principle from the sovereignty of the states of the United States or of other federations. Sovereignty, they assert, has always been historically conditioned and susceptible of legal limitation, however much those limitations may differ in degree. They have been confident that international law would eventually bring the sovereignty of nations under control as the Constitution of the

United States, with, it is true, the travail of a great Civil War, eventually brought the sovereignty of the individual states under control.

To Francis of Victoria in the sixteenth century, to Grotius in the seventeenth, to Wolff in the eighteenth, to Westlake in the nineteenth, to Politis, Lauterpacht, Hudson, and many other jurists in the twentieth century, the trend toward a federal world was clear, as was the task of international lawyers in clarifying its framework and perfecting the techniques for its successful functioning.

There were, however, skeptics. Historians looking over the post-Renaissance centuries more frequently stressed the struggle for power than the evolution of a law-abiding world society. Bishop Stubbs, for example, the historian of the medieval British constitution, justified his preference for medieval history by the greater respect for law which it exhibited. He regarded the study of right and law as "more wholesome" than the study of forces or ideas.[2] He wrote:

The Middle Ages proper, the centuries from the year 1000 to the year 1500 . . . . were ages of legal growth, ages in which the idea of right, as embodied in law, was the leading idea of statesmen, and the idea of rights, justified or justifiable by the letter of the law, was a profound influence with politicians.[3]

[2] William Stubbs, *Seventeen Lectures on the Study of Medieval and Modern History* (Oxford: Clarendon Press, 1887), p. 240.

[3] *Ibid.*, p. 211.

In contrast the "foremost idea of the three centuries that intervene between the year 1500 and the year 1800 . . . . was the idea of the balance of power." It is the "principle which gives unity to the political plot of modern European history."[4] The nineteenth century was, he thought, governed by "ideas," especially the idea of nationality, rather than by either rights or forces. "Out of the crucible, out of the fiery furnace, against the will of the potent actors, as if by a law that may not be broken, the victory of the idea is rapidly being realized," he wrote in 1880, suggesting incidentally that ideas of Pan-Slavism, of internationalism, and of nihilism seemed to be rising to combat the idea of nationalism.[5]

Politicians of the modern period have generally borne out the historian's generalization. They have preferred power or ideas to law as instruments in the field of world politics. While some statesmen of our generation, like Secretary Hull and Secretary Root, both presidents of the American Society of International Law, have frequently insisted upon the importance of law in world affairs and have urged governments to observe it and peoples to understand it, more frequently statesmen have spoken of international law with slight respect or have ignored it altogether. Lord Salisbury said

[4] *Ibid.*, p. 225.          [5] *Ibid.*, p. 239.

in 1887: "International law depends generally upon the prejudices of writers of textbooks. It can be enforced by no tribunal, and therefore to apply to it the phrase 'law' is to some extent misleading."[6]

The dynamic practitioners of world politics have often agreed in act, if not in utterance, with Machiavelli when he said, "A prince ought to have no other aim or thought, nor select anything else for his study, than war and its rules and discipline; for this is the sole art that belongs to him who rules."[7] Hamilton expressed a similar opinion when, in emphasizing the difficulties of federations, he wrote:

> There is in the nature of sovereign power an impatience of control, that disposes those who are invested with the exercise of it to look with an evil eye upon all external attempts to restrain or direct its operations. . . . . Power controlled or abridged is almost always the rival and enemy of that power by which it is controlled or abridged.[8]

The skepticism of historians and politicians in regard to the influence of international law in modern history has been shared by lawyers. As is well known, private law jurists are wont to deal with international law somewhat patronizingly. That law is well enough for departments of political science but hardly to be given a place in the regular

[6] House of Lords Debate, July 26, 1887.

[7] *The Prince*, trans. W. K. Marriot (Everyman's ed.; New York: E. P. Dutton & Co., 1908), chap. xiv, p. 115.

[8] *The Federalist*, ed. Paul L. Ford (New York: Henry Holt & Co., 1898), No. 15, p. 94.

law-school curriculum. This idea gained support in the nineteenth century through the writings of John Austin, who defined law as the command of a political superior to political inferiors. Since the sovereign nations admitted no political superiors he concluded there was no international law. He was ready to admit the existence of the subject under the name "public international morality," but by thus naming it in a materialistic and utilitarian world he consigned it to a position of comparative unimportance.[9] It is true, courts no less august than the Supreme Court in the United States and the Judicial Committee of the Privy Council in England asserted that international law is law, though, they added, a law subject to be overruled in the domestic forum by the highest legislative authority of the nation.[10]

The international lawyers might have ignored the attacks of historians, politicians, and private-law lawyers by escaping to the ivory tower of pure thought, but attacks by internationalists themselves could not be evaded in either theory or practice. In the middle of the eighteenth century Em-

---

[9] *Lectures on Jurisprudence*, I (5th ed.; London, 1911), 173 and 226. John Bassett Moore believes the Austinian doctrine adversely affected attitudes of courts toward international law; see *International Law and Some Current Illusions* (New York: Macmillan Co., 1924), p. 283.

[10] The Paquette Habana, 175 U.S. 677 (1900); The Zamora, 2 A.C. 77 (1916).

merich Vattel, in one of the most widely read books on international law—a book included in the classics of that subject—denied the existence of a world society and attempted to rest positive international law on the sole foundation of agreement. With this hypothesis, the rule requiring that agreements be observed must itself rest on agreement; consequently, it offers no support for the ultimate agreement. Binding law must have some firmer foundation than the will of the person subject to the law.

It is not surprising that Vattel, writing in the middle of the Seven Years' War, should have been unable to find the society of nations, the *Civitas maxima*, upon whose collective will his predecessor, Christian Wolff, had rested the authority of international law. It is, however, more surprising that Vattel should have thought it worth while to write about international law at all when his theory led him to the conviction that a superior society "is not to be thought of as between nations. Each independent state," he wrote, "claims to be, and actually is, independent of all the others." Vattel seems not to have realized that his tautology was destructive to the subject which he was discussing, especially when he attributed to "independence" freedom from the judgment—legal or moral—of anyone else."¹ His exposition of the basis of inter-

¹¹ *The Law of Nations*, trans. C. G. Fenwick (Carnegie ed.) Preface, p. 9*a*.

national law justified John Austin's view of the subject and greatly influenced subsequent writers who, like Vattel, lacked the acumen to see that a positivism, which sought to found international law solely on the individual consent of the sovereign states bound, was not law at all.[12]

Whether or not we agree with van Vollenhoven's assertion that Vattel "gave a Judas kiss to Grotius' system,"[13] we cannot deny that international law after his time was more fecund in the production of words than in the control of states. It has produced thousands of tomes in all languages and many judicial opinions, but it could not be said with assurance that it ever deterred a statesman from initiating war or embarking upon a conquest when "reasons of state" suggested such a course. It influenced diplomatic etiquette, the terminology of treaties, the practices of neutrality and maritime capture, and the decisions of courts in matters without great political importance, but rarely did it affect public opinion in a time of crisis or the high politics of sovereign states.

It is not surprising that, with this record before him, so good an internationalist as Sir Alfred Zim-

[12] H. Lauterpacht, *The Function of Law in the International Community* (Oxford: Clarendon Press, 1933), pp. 3 and 7.

[13] Cornelius van Vollenhoven, *The Three Stages in the Evolution of the Law of Nations* (The Hague: M. Nijhoff, 1919), p. 28.

mern could say at the Harris Institute four years ago:

> This motley and haphazard collection of rules is in no sense a system of world-law or even a faint adumbration of such a system. It suffers indeed from two inherent and incurable defects that suffice to disqualify at the outset any claim that might be put forward on its behalf as the natural point of departure for a further advance along the road to a system of world-law.[14]

The two defects to which Sir Alfred referred were the lack of hold which international law had upon the loyalty of more than an "infinitesimal proportion" of the world's people and the indiscrimination with which it admitted all states, good and bad, advanced and backward, to its sway. Sir Alfred, however, does not explain how world order can be achieved without law or how such a law can avoid dealing with bad states as well as good. He implies that a wholly new law must be developed among the free or "welfare states" alone, without adequately explaining how heavily armed "power states" outside this legal community can be prevented from trying to upset it.

Why has the fair picture of the evolution of the great society under the influence of international law toward a world federation of peace, justice, and

[14] Q. Wright (ed.), *Neutrality and Collective Security* (Chicago: University of Chicago Press, 1936), p. 21. Other statements of Zimmern to similar effect are quoted by N. A. M. Mackenzie in *Proceedings, American Society of International Law* (New York, 1938), p. 7.

order been observed with such jaundiced eyes by so many competent observers? Its most earnest adherents cannot deny a measure of truth in these strictures. By examining international law, both in theory and in operation, perhaps the reasons for its defects may be discovered—surely the first step toward remedy. These defects can be divided according as they spring from external conditions or from internal inconsistencies.

Among the former are (1) the persistence of the idea of empire, (2) the recurrent potentialities of military power, (3) the great diversity of the members of the family of nations, (4) the irresponsibility of third parties in times of crisis, and (5) the comparative adequacy of the balance of power while Britain was able to serve as the balancer.

1. The Middle Ages had an idea of world order —an idea, as Stubbs pointed out, manifested in a well-integrated body of law, but it was not a federal idea. The ghost of ancient Rome lingered on, and pope and emperor contended for the supreme position with all other human authorities ranged below in a descending hierarchy. The Bull, *Unum sanctuum*, of Boniface VIII and the *De monarchia* of Dante, both written in the first decade of the fourteenth century, marked the culminating expositions of order by the imperial method. It is true that about the same time Pierre Dubois expounded an ordered Europe through a federation

of princes, but his notion was far less in the atmosphere of the time.

While the federal idea grew through successive expositions by internationalists, the notion of world peace through a hierarchical order did not easily die. Charles V tried to apply it in the sixteenth century as did Louis XIV in the seventeenth, Napoleon in the nineteenth, and Hitler in the twentieth. The notion of world order through federalism with power flowing from the bottom up, inherent in the Grotian system of international law, is not easy to reconcile with the imperial idea which conceives of power as flowing from the top down, especially when the latter idea was more frequently manifested in the internal structure of the states—members of the family of nations. Federalism is the organization of consent in the international field, but people were more familiar with the organization of violence than with the organization of consent in the national field. Consequently, the idea of a world hierarchically organized by conquest was easy for the public to grasp, and the repeated efforts to realize that idea conflicted with both the popular appreciation and the practical efficiency of the system of international law.

2. The modern period was ushered in by effective utilization of gunpowder, enabling Renaissance monarchs to batter down feudal castles that had long been invulnerable and to establish nation-

al states. These states preserved peace and freed trade in larger areas, thus increasing economic efficiency. This practical achievement revived faith in the power of armies as instruments of politics.

While at times the practice of arms appeared to reach a stalemate from which no one could benefit: the successes of Cromwell, Louis XIV, and Frederick with highly disciplined infantry; the successes of Napoleon with the propaganda of revolution and the strategy of forced marches; the successes of Grant and Moltke in utilizing railroads for war; and the most recent achievements of Hitler with the co-ordination of airplanes, tanks, and infantry have kept alive the expectation among energetic leaders that a wider political order might be achieved by violence. Force in defiance of law achieved the political results desired, and consequently law was at a discount. Had the defensive in war gained the upper hand permanently as it often threatened to do, had military inventors been less active, statesmen might have despaired of war and might have come to agree with Grotius that "the state which transgresses the laws of nature and of nations cuts away also the bulwarks which safeguard its own future peace."[15] But these things did not happen. Force has often been successful, might has made right. The nemesis which may

[15] *The Law of War and Peace: Prolegomena*, trans. F. W. Kelsey (Carnegie ed.; Oxford: Clarendon Press, 1925), sec. 18, p. 16.

eventually overtake the lawbreaking state has proved too distant greatly to affect the conduct of governments.

Today one would be more hesitant than was W. E. Hall in 1889 to say:

> Looking back over the last couple of centuries, we see international law at the close of each fifty years in a more solid position than that which it occupied at the beginning of the period. Progressively it has taken firmer hold, it has extended its sphere of operation.[16]

Yet this optimistic attitude characterized most jurists in the 1920's,[17] a fact well to remember while under the present overshadowing influence of military events and one which justifies Hall's further statement:

> Times in which international law has been seriously disregarded, have been followed by periods in which the European conscience has done penance by putting itself under straighter obligations than those which it before acknowledged.[18]

3. The members of the family of nations always displayed a considerable variety of culture, language, and tradition, but this diversity increased as nations of Eastern Europe, of the Moslem world,

---

[16] *A Treatise on International Law*, Preface to 3d ed. (8th ed.; Oxford: Clarendon Press, 1924), p. xxv.

[17] Q. Wright, *Research in International Law since the War* (Washington: Carnegie Endowment for International Peace, 1930), pp. 2 and 24.

[18] *Op. cit.*, p. xxvi.

and of the Far Eastern world were admitted, as well as the self-determining colonies in North and South America, Australia, New Zealand, and South Africa. Cultural differences and geographical differences, carrying with them divergent interests and ideas of justice, have made it difficult to frame common rules satisfactory to all. International law, in seeking to facilitate the coexistence of very diverse nations and cultures could hardly develop rules at the same time flexible enough to satisfy every state's sentiment of justice and detailed enough to maintain order. The dual function of preserving the independence and individuality of the parts along with the unity and solidarity of the whole is difficult in all federal systems, but especially so in one embracing such a variety of nations as does the world community.

4. The Greek lawgiver, Solon, is reported to have said that in a well-ordered community "any wrongs that are done to individuals are resented and redressed by the other members of the community as promptly and as vigorously as if they themselves were personal sufferers."[19] Grotius recommended that states intervene in the presence of wrongdoing to their neighbors. If states had been inclined to do so upon ascertaining the first acts of lawless violence, the possibilities of utilizing new weapons for

[19] Plutarch *Solon* § 18; quoted in Grotius, *op. cit.*, I, c. v, § 2, p. 164.

successful aggression might have been reduced. But states, not directly affected, sheltered often by natural barriers of mountains or sea, have hesitated to assume the risk involved in such intervention. They have preferred the immediate safety of neutrality, without realizing that, in a world society without an organized executive and police force, neutrality if practiced by all makes a world safe for aggression. The strong state can always conquer a weak neighbor if all the world remains neutral. Between the states expanding aggressively and the irresponsible neutrals there have been few ready to support law, and indeed it is to be feared that when interventions did occur support of law was more likely to be a pretext than a purpose. In a society composed exclusively of gangsters and nonvoters, law and order could hardly be expected to flourish.

5. Under these conditions one may well ask how did civilization survive at all. It might be supposed that the situation would have become so desperate that states would have been driven to unite to give order to the world. During the seventeenth and eighteenth centuries there were indeed voices like Crucé, Sully, Penn, St. Pierre, Rousseau, and Kant who, inspired by the supposed grand design of Henry IV, expounded the virtues of a more perfect federal union of Europe to maintain law and to prevent war. These voices might have been heeded had not a moderate degree of order been

achieved through the British success in maintaining the balance of power in Europe and a fairly adequate police overseas. With a dominant navy and priority as the world's banker and industrial producer, British statesmen, intent on promoting commerce and liberty, were able to maintain the *pax Britannica* through much of two centuries.

British statesmen began to base their policy on sea power and the maintenance of European equilibrium at the end of the seventeenth century. While there were wars Britain, operating from the secure aloofness of her island base, could localize them and, by means of alliances, subsidies, economic pressures, and, if necessary, maritime war, prevent any continental power from achieving empire. British energies in this task were severely taxed during the American Revolution and the Napoleonic period, but during the remainder of the two centuries, from the Peace of Utrecht to the Battle of the Marne, the world enjoyed a moderate *pax Britannica* and throve in population, wealth, and liberty as never before.

The decline of the British position in the twentieth century through naval inventions reducing the potency of sea power, through the rise of even greater financial and commercial powers, and finally through the invention of the airplane ended that era and ushered in the period of anarchy in which we live. The *pax Britannica* had given Europe the best two centuries it had had—at least since the *pax Romana* of a millennium and a half earlier—but it had both obscured and augmented the weaknesses of international law.

An international society organized in fact by Britain and the balance of power could give lip service to international law without realizing how weak that law really was. That weakness was realized when, after the first World War, effort was made to organize world federalism in the League of Nations. It is quite possible that the League would have succeeded had all the states, particularly the United States, become members during the period of early enthusiasm. In any case, difficulties would have arisen because of the absence of an adequately developed body of international law.

New institutions require law which is adapted to their functioning and which people are accustomed to respect. American federalism developed on the firm foundations of the common law, but the League of Nations rested upon an international law which few knew, which was full of internal inconsistencies, and which commanded but slight respect. The American default in membership may itself be attributed to the dubious idea of neutrality which had crept into international law. Weakened by this default, by the failure of disarmament, by the rising of trade barriers, and by the great depression, the League tottered with the first determined act of aggression against it by Japan and toppled over when Mussolini and Hitler defied it.

These external difficulties have both caused and been affected by serious internal inconsistencies in international law. The most glaring of these deficiencies are (1) the law's toleration of war and neutrality, (2) its tolerance of the rule that states can be judges in their own controversies, (3) its insistence that only states and not individuals are subjects of international law, and (4) its insistence that no state is bound by a new rule except with its own consent.

All of these inconsistencies flow in part from the lack of effective international organization and are not likely to be remedied without improved international institutions, but, on the other hand, it is doubtful whether effective international institutions can be established unless the law itself is remedied in these respects.

1. Mature systems of law characterize unprovoked acts of violence by a subject of law which is destructive of the rights of another by the word "crime." Violence may in such systems be legitimately employed in self-defense or to prevent or suppress crime. In more primitive legal systems self-help is sometimes permitted against persons guilty of wrongdoing who have been outlawed by appropriate process. Violence is also sometimes employed as a procedural expedient in trials by

battle. Duels of honor may be permitted in which bystanders must be neutral. These latter processes suggest analogies to war, and the persistence of the latter in international law brands that system as primitive.

The modern community of nations, however, differs from primitive society in that it is not governed by relatively unchangeable customs but is highly dynamic. It is progressive in the use of science; its members are sophisticated in the idea of justice and guide their action by policy rather than by custom. Obviously, legal tolerance of violence, which by nature is destructive of rights which the law purports to protect, presents an inconsistency unless such violence is undertaken in necessary defense of rights subject to eventual legal control or under authority of the law itself to prevent or remedy violations.

This inconsistency of war, considered as a self-willed resort to violence for political ends, with the idea of law was recognized in the Middle Ages and by the early international jurists who elaborated distinctions between just and unjust war. But development of the idea of sovereignty and of neutrality, as well as the growing power of states, led to an abandonment of this distinction, leaving war as an almost unlimited power to destroy the rights of others by force while third states were free to remain impartially neutral. Apart from the inconsistency of the privileges of war and neutrality with the idea of law, the increasing gravity of war, as military invention advanced and world economy became more integrated, aroused popular interest in the problem. This led to international legislation looking toward its elimination, mildly in the Hague Convention of 1899, more explicitly in the League of Nations Covenant, and completely in the Pact of Paris. Procedures, however, were not provided for assuring that practice would accord with the new law thus proclaimed.

2. Early in the seventeenth century Lord Coke held that an act of parliament which made a man judge in his own case was so contrary to natural law that it was null and void.[20] The reasons were later given by John Locke, who said: "It is easy to be imagined that he who was so unjust as to do his brother an injury, will scarce be so just as to condemn himself for it."[21] Yet Locke admitted that sovereign princes were in the state of nature which permitted the exercise of this prerogative, and, according to the Permanent Court of International Justice, it is still a basic principle of international law that no state can be subjected to any jurisdiction without its own consent.[22] Treaties of compul-

[20] Dr. Bonham's Case, 8 Co. Rep. 107a, 114a (1600).

[21] *Of Civil Government*, II, chap. ii, sec. 13 (*Works* [London, 1801], V, 345).

[22] Eastern Carelia Case, Per. Ct. Int. Just., Ser. B, No. 5 (1923).

sory arbitration and the optional clause of the statute of the Permanent Court have, it is true, resulted in many obligations for such submission, but usually with qualifications. Impartial application of law in all controversies seems to be an essential element of a coherent system of law. The existence of a rule in international law denying such application and permitting each state to judge both itself and the other party in the controversy is not only inconsistent with the rule of international law giving foreign sovereigns immunity from national jurisdiction but is glaringly inconsistent with the idea of law. The existence of this rule is a major justification to those who deny that international law is really law.

3. Most writers assert that only states are subject to international law. Individuals are bound by the municipal law which, springing from different sources, may conflict with international law. While it is recognized that a state owes a duty to other states whose nationals are in its territory to respect basic rights of such aliens, yet it owes no duty under international law in respect to its own nationals. It may treat them as barbarously as it wishes and may deprive them of all liberties. As a result, under international law man seems to exist for the state, not the state for man. This situation, hostile to democratic theory, is also hostile to an effective international law. If a state can deprive its

nationals of all freedom of communication with the outside world, it can frustrate the possibility of a world public opinion which alone could sustain an effective international law. Governments, dependent for their existence upon a national public, cannot be expected to observe international obligations when that public demands otherwise. Furthermore, it is to be expected that the public will frequently demand otherwise if it is deprived of the opportunity to hear the voice of those whose rights will be infringed by the action in question. Even without such deprivation the average man is not usually interested in foreign opinion. For this reason even democratic governments are prone to neglect international obligations. Autocratic governments, sustaining themselves on the principle of absolutism, may be expected to neglect international obligations whenever expediency suggests.

Furthermore, coercive sanctions, even if supported by the collective force of the community of nations, if directed against a powerful state resemble war rather than police. An effective system of federal law is enforced, not against states as such, but by the nullification of conflicting state law in cases brought to court by individuals, or by the coercion of individuals or officials within the state. Thus the recognition that individuals are subject to international law, are protected in certain rights by that law even against their own state, and are responsible under that law for breaches of its principles irrespective of state legislation would greatly strengthen the application of international law. Some jurists have asserted the personality of individuals as subjects of international law, and certain international institutions have accorded direct access to individuals. Further developments of this principle, however, appear to be essential, if international law is to provide the basis for an adequate world federation.

4. While most writers on international law trace its binding force to the general consensus of the members of the world community and do not require evidence that each state has expressly consented to the existing rules, yet this latter evidence is considered necessary to prove that a new rule is binding upon a state. International legislation can be effected only by treaties which bind only the parties. Thus the practical application of the *liberum veto*, so destructive in the old Polish diet, is equally destructive to the law in the highly dynamic family of nations. The difficult process of legislation through multipartite treaties has proved slow, but not impossible, as a means for enacting the law required to regulate new agencies such as air traffic, radio, and new conditions arising from more rapid travel and communication, such as postal services, health, labor standards, etc. The difficulties of this cumbersome process of legisla-

tion have, however, proved insuperable for modifying established rules which no longer conform to the requirements of justice. Thus the rule which extends the domestic jurisdiction of a state to complete control of its tariffs, money, and armaments permits a state, under modern conditions, to injure its neighbors tremendously without transgressing the law. While judicial legislation utilizing such equitable principles as that no one should use his own so as to injure another might, if there were compulsory jurisdiction, remedy some such abuses; an adequate system of legislation abandoning the requirement of unanimity seems essential if international law is to be kept abreast of justice in the modern dynamic world.

In reviewing the defects of international law which flow both from its external environment and from its internal inconsistencies, it has not been intended to excuse either the law or the lawyers. International law has at the moment failed in its task. The great opportunity offered the world in the 1920's and 1930's to organize national autonomy under law in an effective world federation was wasted. That opportunity may not return for generations. Democracy and liberty may perish even in the corners where they remain today, for it is clear that under modern conditions democracy cannot survive in a jungle world. Democracy cannot exist without law. Liberty of the person and of the group, which is the essence of democracy, is continually threatened by the Scylla of arbitrary authority and the Charybdis of social disintegration. A common law defining the limits of liberty for each, in order to maximize liberty for all, is the only solution. Now that states are economically interdependent and all vulnerable to new weapons of war in the hands of despots, that law must be world wide if democracy is to survive anywhere. The prime failure of democracy has been its failure to organize the world for peace. That failure sprang in part from a failure to develop rules and principles of international law which were internally consistent and adequate to the task.

Today international law, international organization, and, with them, democracy and liberty are receding before the shattering blows of the new despotism, intent on organizing the world as an imperial hierarchical order in which democracy has no place. If a different system of world federation, in which democracy and liberty alone can survive in our shrinking world, is to emerge, a more perfect international law must be developed to sustain it.

Under that law violence must, except for defense or for police, be illegal; war and neutrality as legal statuses must disappear; states as well as persons must be subject to the jurisdiction of impartial tribunals; individuals must be subject directly to international law which must penetrate within the state to protect the fundamental rights of man and to prevent basic transgressions by individuals and public officers; practical legislative procedures must be devised to accommodate law to changing conditions and ideas of justice.

International law has struggled toward such goals, clearly perceived by its architects five centuries ago, but its environment has often been adverse and its protagonists have not always been wise.

In the grave trials through which international law is now passing its true character, as the system of ideas which alone can make the world safe for nationality, for democracy, for humanity, and for liberty, must be more widely understood. Law ultimately rests on the support of public opinion, and international law can rest only on the support of world-wide public opinion. That support, however, will not be forthcoming unless publicists and educators give their best efforts to the task, unless the jurists continually re-examine the sources of law and interpret its rules and principles with an understanding of ever changing needs, and unless the statesmen continually labor at the reconstruction of world institutions which can assure the application and development of its rules and principles in a world of varied and dynamic nations.

# THE UNITED STATES AND WORLD ORDER

*By* J. Fred Rippy
Professor of American History

# THE UNITED STATES AND WORLD ORDER

WITH reference to the European segment of the world order the United States has followed the policy of political isolation during most of its national existence. That policy was formulated during the struggle for independence, in spite of the fact that the struggle was effectively assisted by France. In respect to Europe, there was no departure from the platform of isolationism for more than a hundred years. Important deviations began only with the turn of the nineteenth century.

Such a policy must have been firmly grounded in national sentiments and convictions; otherwise, it would not have been pursued so consistently. Its emotional and rational foundations may be summed up as follows: (1) the memory of unpleasant experiences during the Colonial period when the inhabitants of the Thirteen Colonies were dragged into every European war; (2) the belief that the interests of Europe and the United States were not parallel; (3) the conviction that the political system and moral standards of the United States were superior; (4) the fear that American leaders would be no match for the subtle schemers of Europe, who would involve the nation in Europe's endless strife; (5) the belief that an isolated neutrality would enable the United States to profit from Europe's inevitable conflicts by expanding its commerce, increasing its territorial domain in North America, and regulating the conduct of the discordant European nations in respect to the New World; (6) the conviction that geography—three thousand miles of ocean—decreed both the wisdom and the possibility of adhering to such a policy.

Temptations to depart from the policy were numerous. The nation stood on the isolationist platform, but it often stood there besieged. Among the besieging forces were both economic interests and fundamental ideals.

The material influences tending to drive the nation from its position were the expansion of its trade and eventually the export of its capital. But apparently the close connection between foreign commerce and investments and political involvement was not fully realized. The people hoped to have their profits and their isolation too.

The psychological or idealistic forces tending to drive the nation from the isolationist platform consisted of deep convictions regarding domestic politics and the conduct of foreign relations. The United States was devoted to democracy as the best system of government and to peaceful adjustment as the proper method of settling international disputes. It was opposed to absolutism and despotism, and it was opposed to the use of force as an instrument of international politics. Although the nation had its wars, the people were nevertheless devotees of peace; they believed that nations should settle their difficulties without resort to violence.

Enthusiasm for the democratic way of life was expressed in respect to every popular movement in Europe from the French Revolution of 1789 to the overthrow of the Spanish king in 1873 and the downfall of the Hapsburgs and Hohenzollerns in 1918. The tendency of this enthusiasm was to drive the nation from its platform of isolationism and cause it to take part in European political affairs.

The organized peace movement in the United States, which dates from 1815, tended to propel the nation in precisely the same direction. Between 1815 and 1860 American pacifists often collaborated with pacifists across the Atlantic in efforts to preserve the peace of Europe. These early interventions were private attempts at pacification in which the government of the United States evinced little concern. By 1899, however, the American peace organizations were strong enough to become largely responsible for the official participation of the United States in the first peace conference at The Hague. During the next few years their strength increased so much that even a combative

statesman like Theodore Roosevelt could not ig-
nore their importance. He complained of their op-
position to large expenditures for armaments, but
he also exerted himself to limit the scope and
shorten the duration of the Russo-Japanese War,
urged the submission of certain international disputes to the Hague Court, intervened in the Moroc-
can crisis of 1905–6, and helped to sponsor the second peace conference at The Hague. In thus acting to preserve the peace of Europe, Roosevelt was
doubtless influenced by a number of motives. It is
likely that one of them was the desire to appeal to
the pacifists and win their support.

The intervention of the United States in the war
of 1914–18 was the one great departure from the
isolationist policy. On that occasion two fundamental ideals and a concept of national interest
converged to form a mighty impulse to act. The
nation's economic ties were with Great Britain and
her allies. But this alone does not account for the
intervention. The nation deeply resented German
methods of war, and at least some of its leaders
feared that a German victory might imperil the
security of the United States. Yet not even these
three motives combined are sufficient to explain the
entrance of the United States into the war. From
the viewpoint of the American people it was in a
very real sense a war to end war and make the
world safe for democracy; it was the militant ex-

pression of devotion to peace and the democratic way of life.

For more than a century, at least, the policy of isolation tended to promote the interests of the nation. By virtue of its aloofness from European politics and because of Europe's strife, the United States was free to have its way in the New World. A contentious Europe was able neither to prevent the expansion of the territorial domain of the United States nor to resist the regulation under the Monroe Doctrine of European political procedures in the New World. These were two important advantages of the isolation policy foreseen by Thomas Jefferson and Alexander Hamilton at an early date. And there was a third. The United States reaped an enormous commercial advantage from Europe's conflicts. It is true that the British navy was a factor in the enforcement of the Monroe Doctrine against the powers of Continental Europe. But British policy in respect to the territorial integrity and the national independence of the Latin-American states was largely the expression of commercial and political rivalry with European powers. It was mainly the result of the strife of Europe, although it was doubtless motivated in part by liberal tendencies.

With reference to the world beyond Europe, isolation sentiment has been a less influential factor in determining the policy of the United States. In the

Far East and the Pacific area its policy has been characterized by a measure of entanglement and collaboration with European powers and Japan. Illustrations of departure from the isolationist platform in this vast region are familiar to every student of international relations. The policy of William H. Seward in respect to China, the Samoan Condominium, the Open Door Notes, the financial consortiums, and various recent pacts will be recalled without effort. The Founding Fathers recommended no policy regarding the politics of the Pacific area, and the traders and capitalists of the United States were eager for access to the vast markets for goods and investments envisaged in China. When these glowing prospects failed to materialize, national interest in China decreased, but the disposition to take part in far eastern politics by no means disappeared.

The one grand intervention of the United States in Europe finally resulted in oppressive disillusionment. But disillusionment was not the cause of the withdrawal. It was caused by domestic politics. One of our great parties—a party whose outstanding leaders were the first to insist that we enter the war of 1914–18—sought to win an election by stirring up the residue of isolationism. The effort succeeded and the nation returned to its isolationist platform. In strict justice it must be noted that the Republicans, according to the view of some historians, were influenced in part by the appalling terms of the Versailles Treaty. It is likely, however, that they were actuated mainly by partisan motives.

Regarding the effects of this withdrawal from Europe the experts cannot wholly agree. The majority will probably contend that its immediate result was the increase of the "fear complex" in France and the occupation of the Ruhr, followed by inflation in Germany and the ruin of the lower middle class with all the suffering, frustration, and disorder that this produced. But who can prove that inflation would not have been resorted to by Germany in any event sooner or later as a means of wiping out the stupendous cost of the war?

After this catastrophe the situation in Germany and Europe rapidly improved. To the reconstruction of Germany, as well as of other war-harassed countries, the United States made a large contribution. The American holders of billions of defaulted and repudiated bonds—some two billions of them German bonds—will regretfully testify to that immense contribution. In 1925 Europe entered the era of Locarno. If the withdrawal of the United States from the new world order of 1920 was unfortunate, recovery from that misfortune seemed to be achieved.

But the Locarno period lasted only six years. For its termination it is asserted that the world economic depression was the main cause, although the militaristic spirit and the political philosophy of Germany may have been more important. It is not contended that the United States was solely responsible for the world depression. Yet it is urged that a combination of the American tariff laws of 1922 and 1930 and the American attempt to collect the war debts was an important contributing factor. Perhaps this is true. Yet the debt situation was novel, and what other government would have desisted from the effort to collect the sums other nations owed it? Moreover, when the final European collapse threatened, it was the United States that took the lead in arranging the moratorium which meant the abandonment of reparations, and for the United States nothing but tokens and soon not even these. As for the postwar tariffs, the United States took the lead in protectionism. But this was again the fault of the party that repudiated the new world order in 1919 and after; and who can be certain that the nations of Europe would not have descended into the calamitous era of trade barriers even if the United States had not led the way?

If the United States, chastened by the world economic collapse, had returned to the League of Nations in 1930 or 1931, would it have been able to turn the world away from the fateful course that has brought humanity to its darkest era? To believe this will require enormous optimism. Although out of the League, the United States began a period of more willing collaboration in certain matters as early as 1928 with the signing of the Kellogg Pact. Call this pact a hollow gesture if you like; it indicated in the United States a developing concern in the peace of the world. The events that followed need no elaboration. As the nations descended step by step to the tragic present, few of them were more willing to apply economic sanctions and the sanction of refusal to recognize conquest than was the United States. The government at Washington even co-operated with England and France in one of their serious mistakes. It followed their lead in dealing with Spain.

The most appalling errors were made in respect to Germany during the years following 1933. Would the course of events have been different if the United States had been a member of the League? This is a question more appropriately answered by philosophers. The historian will respond by asking another question: Would the representatives of the United States at Geneva have been less paralyzed by the fear of the revolt of the masses and less inclined to build up Adolf Hitler as a bulwark against communism and radicalism than were those of other nations? If this question can be answered with a confident affirmative, then the absence of the United States from the League must be deeply lamented.

Let it be supposed that the United States was a member of the League in 1938 and that its representatives at Geneva were disposed to save Czechoslovakia. Could they have obtained the consent of Congress to the dispatch of an expeditionary force to Europe in order to hold Hitler in check even if such a force had been ready?

Surely doubt is justified on this point. Already an overwhelming resurgence of isolationism had taken control of the Congress and the people of the United States. Most of the Democratic lawmakers, even, had become isolationists. Practically the whole nation had rushed back to the old platform. By 1938 the storm-cellar legislation had been written on the statute books. In the circumstances, it is extremely doubtful whether Franklin Roosevelt and his Geneva delegation, if one had been there, could have made commitments that would have transformed appeasement into defiance.

This resurgence of isolation sentiment in the United States may have been significant. It has been contended that it was a green light to Hitler. By the provisions of the so-called neutrality legislation and especially by its arms embargo the world order had been made as safe for aggressors as Congress could make it. But England and France could have bought armaments from the United States before the war of 1939 began, and after its beginning the arms embargo was repealed. That phase of the matter was therefore of little importance. The significant factor is this: England and France were asleep.

It will be argued that the primary consideration, as far as the United States was concerned, was its display of isolationist indifference in the presence of the approaching crisis. The isolationist indifference is a fact. It was based on a great disillusionment regarding the excursion of 1917–19 into European politics. It arose not merely from the large financial losses occasioned by the war and its aftermath of attempted reconstruction. It was also founded upon the conviction in many quarters that the war and all modern wars were the work of international financiers and manufacturers of munitions. The conduct of both was investigated in the 1930's, and the conclusion was hastily drawn from the record. But more important than this, perhaps, the disillusionment was in large measure the result of a loss of faith in the organization of economic society then prevailing. It was an outgrowth of the depression.

Hitherto it had been commonly assumed that a fair apportionment of jobs—namely, a fair division of labor—and a fair distribution of the common produce of labor, capital, and management were automatically effected by the system of laissez faire and free contract. In the 1930's many people reached the conviction that the system was no longer practical. The debacle of 1929 and after, with revelations of mistakes and misconduct on the part of certain bankers and corporation executives, caused a loss of faith in the old system. It was tantamount to the loss of a social religion. The very foundation of the old economic order was threatened. Men began to advocate a planned economy. Some of the procedures of totalitarianism seemed plausible and inevitable. As in Europe, class bitterness and class interests tended to smother the national spirit and blind men to the significance of the peril that was developing in Germany, Italy, and Japan. Force was being substituted rapidly for reason and adjustment. Conquerors were already on the march. Yet the minds of men were fixed on domestic grievances. The totalitarians saw the confusion and stimulated it. They concluded that the democracies, including the United States, held no convictions for which they were willing to fight.

These economic problems and the loss of faith in laissez faire and the free market as well as in other moral values strengthened isolationism. There developed a longing for refuge in the faith of the Founding Fathers not merely in economics but in politics. Thomas Jefferson became popular, and never was Washington's farewell address so frequently quoted. Americans did not succeed in reverting to the old economic system, but it was easy to return to Washington's advice on international relations. The losses and frustrations of 1917–19, convictions regarding the economic causes of war, and belief in the efficacy of a planned economy for the United States, strengthened perhaps by the hope of effecting the economic integration of the Western Hemisphere, drove the nation back to its isolationist platform. Franklin D. Roosevelt, after appearing at first to approve the swing toward extreme isolationism, finally revealed his dissent. Cordell Hull and a few of his aides in the State Department stood almost alone among members of the national government in their devotion to internationalism during the whole of the post-depression period. When the second Roosevelt came at last firmly to Hull's support, the two were held in check by Congress and national sentiment, and already it was late.

In 1937 and after, Roosevelt and Hull scolded and warned the aggressors, but they had no means of enforcing their profound disapproval except by measures short of war. And the prudence of even these devices was seriously questioned in many quarters.

So much by way of tribute to the historians of the Harris Institute of 1940. This record has been surveyed in order to explain the attitude of the United States toward the world order since the birth of the nation. But, in surveying the record, I have done more than that. I have expressed doubt regarding the importance of our role in world affairs even if the United States had been a member of the League. The unerring wisdom of American leaders if the nation had chosen to follow the Wilsonian course must not be too readily assumed. Neither must its power to shape European affairs be taken for granted. One has here not merely the question of what is desirable but the question of what is possible. If I have presented a mistaken view, I am sure that subsequent round tables will not fail to correct it. In any event, it can hardly be denied that this nation is unlikely to play a larger part in the establishment and maintenance of the world order envisaged by many members of this Institute until its convictions and sentiments are profoundly changed. And, for the present, its capacity to shape any world order is limited by its lack of military equipment.

If the Nazis completely triumph in the war now in progress, there is grave danger that Europe's strife will cease to shield the Americas as in the past. No conqueror has ever subdued and held in subjection for long such a vast area as Hitler has dominated and may succeed in dominating. But it would be very dangerous to rely on history's repetitions; no conqueror has ever possessed such a war machine and such instruments of terror. Neither can the United States depend upon an immediate war between Germany and the Soviet Union. In all probability the totalitarians will fight it out among themselves some day, but they may postpone the gigantic conflict until they have tried to despoil the United States and its neighbors. Nor is it safe to cherish the hope that the Nazis may be satiated by acquisitions nearer home. Hitler's objective may not be world revolution and world domination as represented by Hermann Rauschning, but the rich raw materials and the immense food reservoir of Latin America may resemble the answer to a Nazi's prayer. First the Monroe Doctrine may be smashed, and then bases established for an attack on the United States. The Americas may soon confront a grave peril.

Moreover, such divergent political ideologies and economic systems as those of the United States and Germany are bound to become immediately and dangerously competitive. It is the policy of the United States not to recognize the fruits of conquest, and the United States is refusing to permit the Nazis to seize the American deposits and investments of the victims of aggression. The United States will try to prevent the Nazis from capturing the Latin-American markets not merely for economic reasons but for vastly more important political reasons. The United States will fight to protect the territory and independence of Latin America as well as to shield Canada, either as a part of the British Empire or as an independent state. Hitler has been denounced from one end of this country to the other. How can there be peace between the United States and Nazi Germany?

We have no world order. We have a house divided. We have the totalitarian despotisms and the democracies, which will soon be confined to the Americas if Great Britain fails to survive. Unless Hitler confronts revolt within his expanding *Lebensraum* or is drawn into war with a rival despot, the future is not bright for the Americas. Only by a supreme effort will the American nations achieve preparedness for defense, adjust themselves to the momentous economic reorganization of Europe, and avoid a perilous decline of living standards. Only by a miracle will democracy and a measure of individual liberty survive on this side of the Atlantic.

What immediate action does the crisis demand? Should England be assisted by all measures short of war? Perhaps so. Should she also be given the benefit of naval convoys for armaments and supplies and even the full assistance of our fleet and air force? In our present state of preparedness one may doubt the wisdom of going that far.

Regarding other policies I feel more certain. The

United States should arm with utmost speed, and neither labor nor capital should be permitted to obtain more than a small profit in the process. The enthusiasm of the people must be aroused for the American way of life. National unity must be achieved on solid economic and spiritual foundations. The United States should collaborate with Latin America in preventing either the American colonies or the American investments of Nazi victims from falling into Hitler's hands. The independent states of the New World should form as rapidly as possible an economic union, to which Canada may be admitted as soon as she requests it. Tariffs and debts should be adjusted at once and every effort made toward a co-operative relief of economic distress in Pan-America. And, finally, the United States should give Latin America every possible and prudent assistance in arming itself for defense. In this crisis time is of the essence, and the most skilful statesmanship is required.

In all the modern tragedy of errors one happy coincidence has occurred. In its origin the Good Neighbor Policy had little connection with the development of the present world crisis. But that policy was adopted at a very opportune moment. The acclaim with which it has been received by Latin-Americans is most fortunate. Prospects for co-operation in their defense and ours seem encouraging. Latin America has a number of dictators, but they are not totalitarians. These countries still consider democracy to be their goal. Despite many deviations in practice, they have not yet lost faith in that system. Moreover, they are ardently nationalistic. They are likely to collaborate with the nation which reveals the greatest respect for their rights and sensibilities. For several years no other country has been so considerate of their interests as has the United States. But the United States must be strong as well as just. Otherwise the Latin-Americans, in desperation, might try to pick the winner. Democracy's sphere may soon be confined to the New World. Here it must be preserved until the millions of Europe find the courage, the means, and the opportunity to recover their lost liberties. In the present world disorder that may be the main task of the United States.

Yet two others are suggested. If Western Europe should confront starvation this winter, should the United States extend relief at the risk of strengthening the very power that most threatens our security? If Great Britain should manage to hold out against the Nazi onslaught for six months or so, should the United States enter the war on her side? These questions are so momentous that I dare not give advice. We may be defeated by attempting too much, but we may also be defeated by attempting too little.[1]

[1] Obviously the scope of the present volume does not permit a documentation of the interpretative survey attempted in this address. Reference will therefore be limited to the following works and bibliographies contained therein: Frank H. Simonds and Brooks Emeny, *The Great Powers in World Politics* (New York, 1939); Thomas A. Bailey, *A Diplomatic History of the American People* (New York, 1940); J. Fred Rippy, *America and the Strife of Europe* (Chicago, 1938).

# THE INSTITUTIONAL REQUIREMENTS
# FOR A MORE STABLE WORLD ORDER

*By* WALTER H. C. LAVES
Associate Professor of Political Science

# THE INSTITUTIONAL REQUIREMENTS
## FOR A MORE STABLE WORLD ORDER

THE subject of this Sixteenth Harris Institute is "The Foundations of a More
Stable World Order." It is concerned,
therefore, with one segment of the much greater
problem of social order which through the centuries
has occupied men's thoughts and for which solu-
tions of many kinds have been proposed at different
times.

In the course of the development of modern nations attention has been focused upon the foundations for a stable order within the national state.
The nature of political organization (whether it
was to be democratic or in some way authoritarian)
and the nature of the economic order (whether freedom of enterprise or some form of socialization
should prevail) have been matters of immediate
concern.

How the world order should be constructed received relatively scant attention except for the occasional blueprints of idealists and scholars. The
stability of the national order came first. Only
gradually was it recognized that completely free
national states might jeopardize the peace of all
and that some of the social problems of modern in-

dustrial society required international co-operation. Thus developed the search for the elements of a world order.

That the world order of the last twenty years lacked stability requires no proof, nor does the fact that there was an intimate relation between the degree of world order and stability and the extent of stability in each state.

This is the background upon which our discussions during this Institute take place as we seek to find the foundations for an order which will be more stable than that we have known to date.[1] Previous lectures have dealt with the broad historical background and with the economic, shipping, and legal aspects of the problem of a world order. It is my function to discuss some institutional aspects of the same problem.

Assuming that by the institutional aspects of a world order we mean primarily the organized machinery of international co-operation, I should like to present this subject in three major divisions: (1) the general character of the institutions operative in the world order to date; (2) the prevailing conceptions which influenced the effectiveness of these institutions; and (3) the prospects for international organization at the present moment.

[1] Some indication of the range of these discussions may be found in Walter H. C. Laves and Francis O. Wilcox, *The Middle West Looks At the War* (Public Policy Pamphlet, No. 32 [Chicago: University of Chicago Press, 1940]).

# INSTITUTIONAL REQUIREMENTS

## I. THE INSTITUTIONS OPERATIVE IN THE
## WORLD ORDER TO DATE

The institutions of international organization existing between 1920 and 1940 were the product of significant changes which had taken place in the modern world during several centuries—changes which made the world a rapidly shrinking area in terms of travel and communication and which were making of the world a single economic, cultural, and social unit. As the world market emerged for the products of national industries, as cultural and social contacts became more firmly meshed, and as peace became indivisible because of the nature and extensive repercussions of war, the need for intergovernmental institutions operating on a worldwide basis became imperative. The institutional problem was one similar to that which appears today in the domestic affairs of this country—a problem of creating governmental administrative areas comparable to the areas in which the new social-economic problems of an urban industrial society develop. (I have in mind particularly those developments in the American social system to which attention has been given by the *Social Trends Report*[2] and by more recent publications of the Na-

[2] *Report of the President's Research Committee on Social Trends: Recent Social Trends in the United States* (New York: McGraw-Hill Book Co., Inc., 1933).

tional Resources Committee[3] dealing with regionalism, metropolitan areas, etc.)

The growth of international institutions was slow despite the pressing needs and in spite of the writings of many jurists and idealists. Indeed, it was not until the last quarter of the nineteenth century that one could see substantial progress. Even then the efforts were halting and the results of doubtful significance. In retrospect, however, these beginnings assume greater importance, since they laid the groundwork for rapid development immediately following the first World War.

The international institutions which thus gradually emerged were of two general types: those concerned with what might be called problems of social welfare and those described by the term "peace machinery." Those dealing with the social welfare were concerned with communication by mail, telegraph, and radio, with waterways, copyrights, navigation, etc. The peace machinery included the Hague Court of Arbitration, the League of Nations, the World Court, etc. The agreements creating these institutions were sometimes universal (signed by nearly all countries), sometimes regional (Pan-American, Far Eastern, Locarno), and sometimes limited to a small number of specified countries. The amount of administrative ma-

[3] See, e.g., *Regional Factors in National Planning* (Washington: U.S. Government Printing Office, 1935).

chinery created varied according to the subject matter and the intentions of the signatories.

The most numerous institutions and the most extensive machinery were created on matters concerning social welfare. These were matters on which there was little controversy and in the regulation of which vital interests did not seem to be affected. Yet it should be pointed out that just as today the regulation of trade is still considered outside the scope of international organizations— still a controversial matter—so in earlier days the regulation of waterways was also considered potentially controversial. Indeed, much of the progress made in regard to the internationalization of waterways was wiped out after 1933 when Hitler saw the national control of rivers and canals as a matter of vital interest. Even today the regulation of the traffic in dangerous drugs, generally recognized as a legitimate object of international control (I think even by the present German government), is still in the realm of international political controversy, in so far as Japan has considered free trade in opium an important weapon in demoralizing Chinese resistance to her conquest of China. But, in general, social welfare machinery developed because more appeared to be gained by co-operation than by insisting upon separate national action. Indeed, it was the recognition of the futility of purely national regulation of postal and telegraphic communication, of disease, of criminal traffic in women and children, and of dangerous drugs which produced these international institutions.

The slowest and least progress was made in creating institutions providing international methods to supplement or replace national methods of handling the issues upon which war and peace depended. Only gradually was the idea accepted that third parties (states or persons other than those immediately concerned in a given dispute) had a legitimate interest in securing a settlement by peaceful means. Even more slowly was it recognized that in certain specific situations the making of final decisions might be removed from foreign offices and left to a tribunal selected for this purpose. Not until after the first World War was it possible to get agreement upon a method of creating a permanent judicial court whose jurisdiction was defined in clear terms and whose judgment was to be final in all cases submitted (barring miscarriages of justice). Throughout this slow evolutionary process it remained a matter of debate what types of questions were suitable for submission to a peaceful settlement by other than purely national means. How slow even this small progress has been may be gathered from a reading of the debates in Congress on the arbitration treaties of 1897, 1905, and 1911 or on the League in 1920 or on the World

Court in 1935. With slight alterations the reasoning used by the opponents of the Anglo-American arbitration project of 1897 would have satisfied the opponents of the World Court in 1935.

The most significant advances in the development of international machinery to deal with social welfare and peace came during the years immediately following the World War. Perhaps it was the tenacious faith of Woodrow Wilson or perhaps the horrors of the war through which the world had just passed—but whatever the cause, nations were prepared in these first years after the armistice of 1918 to set up a comprehensive structure of international co-operation such as the modern world had never seen. Such limited administrative institutions as had existed were largely absorbed into the new framework constructed at Geneva. But to these was added a comprehensive series of bureaus, committees, commissions, and offices which filled the interstices of the old structure and expanded into new areas never before included in international organization.

To man all these new services there were recruited from many nations men and women of ability, industry, and vision. Housed in a palace dedicated to international co-operation and peace, they put life into this limited international government located at Geneva.

In terms of the peace machinery, too, these first

post-war years produced notable advances. Where there had been no international organization before 1914 with powers to inquire into the nature and causes of any threat to the peace of the world and possible bases for its solution, there was created the League of Nations with precisely this power. It was to be a going concern, twenty-four hours a day, ready through its various organs to sense any tremors of impending conflict, to send out for information, to call the disputants to an inquiry, to appoint its own commission of investigation, and to report its findings and recommendations.

In place of the unsatisfactory Hague Court of Arbitration, which was in fact but a panel of candidates for service as judges (if anyone would have them), there was created the world's first permanent judicial court. The long-standing problem of how to select the personnel of such a court was finally resolved by a formula of the American jurist, Elihu Root. Opportunity was also provided for countries to accept compulsory jurisdiction in certain types of cases.

## II. PREVAILING CONCEPTIONS INFLUENCING THE EFFECTIVENESS OF INSTITUTIONS

The number and scope of international organizations described up to this point would be impressive if we were to judge by the standards of the preceding fifty years. This is the temptation to which we usually succumb, when measuring progress in the social world, and it is probably the only way progress can be seen. Unfortunately, however, stability in world affairs depends not merely upon progress in social organization but upon the quality and speed of that progress. What has been said thus far does not touch upon the true nature of these international organizations and does not appraise them in terms of the needs of the times. Moreover, we cannot divorce ourselves and our thinking from the contemporary world. In this world the peace machinery has for the time proved useless, and the League has been in process of steady liquidation as the personnel of more than seven hundred has been reduced to a mere handful.

Were it possible within the limits of this paper, it would be helpful to undertake a detailed examination of the gradual decline in importance and effectiveness of this body of international organizations after 1930. The same end can perhaps be attained, however, by examining briefly the setting in which this international organization was supposed to work.

The need for new institutions of control, as has already been indicated, was created by the great technological changes which followed in the wake of the new scientific spirit of the post-medieval period. The resort to international institutions was the logical answer of a civilization which was attempting in its social life to apply the same rational processes which were increasingly being used outside the field of physical science in which they had had their origin. It was also the logical method to use for a civilization which accepted the philosophy of individualism and which valued the human person above the state. However, the application of rational processes to the creation of social controls was hampered by the religion of nationalism. This modern equivalent of the universal faith of medieval times reached its peak of acceptance just at the time when the need for rational organization was greatest.

The rational approach to the problems of social control placed the individual at the center of the social world, and the democratic doctrine was its logical corollary in the field of politics. It attempted to shape the political institutions in terms of the individual's need and insisted that the state should be responsible to those over whom it governed. This meant a continual reconsideration of the usefulness of political institutions and a reappraisal of their relation to the individual.

In the new economy following the beginnings of the Industrial Revolution this obviously meant the breaking of feudal bonds and the establishment of new areas of social control. Actually this change from smaller to larger areas of social control did not come about simply as the result of democratic and rational thought. Fortunately, the ambitions of kings coincided with the other pressures for larger areas. Thus the national state appeared as a logical step in the process of expansion and liberalization of trade even though the national state set up its own controls in the interest of national power.

In the period since the emergence of the national state the pressure of economic forces and technology has been overwhelmingly toward the creation of a unit of social organization larger than the national state. This might have been secured either (1) through co-operation among existing nations and a voluntary delegation to international government of power over matters of more than national concern (while preserving the cultural peculiarities of peoples within national areas) or (2) through the creation by force of much greater areas of political, economic, and cultural unity. There are indications now that the time for the first alternative on a world-wide basis may have passed; certainly the second alternative is already being tried on the continents of Europe and Asia.

The League of Nations, the Permanent Court of International Justice, and the International Labour Organization are monuments to the application by man of his rational faculties to the problem of interstate relationships. Within these organizations the democratic and rational approach was evidenced by the principles of consultation, conference, conciliation, adjudication, self-determination, administration of backward peoples under mandates, disarmament, and the encouragement of international trade. The Covenant and the statutes of the Court and the International Labour Organization were all steps in this direction.

But expansion of international controls was not rapid enough to insure a stable world order. Consider simply by way of illustration the work of the League of Nations in relation to international trade. If the League's work was to have been of any consequence at all, the League should have been clothed with power. But the League could only recommend ways of encouraging citizens of one country to do business in another; it could only propose how obstacles to the movement of persons and goods could be removed; it could only suggest how international financial payments could be facilitated. In each case application and execution of these findings rested in the hands of the national state, even though the inevitable inaction led to economic and political ruin for all. Virtually the same situation prevailed for all the other agencies concerned with improving the general welfare.

Ten years ago, or even five years ago, one could deplore the overnationalistic policies of states and still have some hope of seeing the solution of international problems by international means. Today, however, the picture has changed. In more than one large part of the world nationalism has been applied with a thoroughness heretofore unknown among national states. Jealous of one another's power and willing to sacrifice the general good for short-lived national independence of action, the states which had it in their power to introduce a new era of internationalism now face a future in which nationalism is carried to its logical conclusion. By resort to violence the new totalitarian states find an easy solution in their dominion for the problems that had plagued the world of independent sovereign states. The problem of trade barriers is solved by removing them forcibly. The all-important question of how to solve disputes between sovereign states without limiting their sovereignty is easily disposed of by removing the states! The terrifying issue of what to do about states which resort to war as an instrument of national policy is resolved by the successful user of this means by disarming all other states and creating a real police force over all. The risks of maintaining peace, so dear to the exponents of isolation as an argument for their policy, have been replaced by such overwhelming risks of making war (even for defense) as no supporter of the Kellogg Pact could ever have hoped for.

These and many other obstacles to stability in the world order based on international co-operation have been easily removed. The method used was force, and the removal of the obstacles to co-operation has been accompanied by the virtual removal of the nations which were supposed to co-operate. With the states has gone also that freedom of thought, expression, and enterprise which were central to a world order based on co-operation.

Thus threatened by weapons partly of their own fashioning, the national democratic states of western Europe and the Americas face an immediate future to which their traditional concepts of international organization no longer apply. Not until their darkest hour had arrived did England and France begin talking of a union with a common government and a common citizenship, and even to the present day there are those in the United States who fondly hold to doctrines of unlimited, irresponsible, isolationist sovereignty, still not seeing that it was these doctrines which brought on the most recent World War.

### III. PROSPECTS FOR INTERNATIONAL ORGANIZATION

Whether the period is ended in which it is still possible to think of the establishment of a functioning system of international co-operation based upon independent national states as we have known them, we cannot tell until the outcome of the present war is known. Until then our speculations concerning future international organization must consider two broad possibilities: The one is that of a world in which order is based on free international co-operation; the other, that of a world in which order is maintained by the domination of a limited number of states.

1. Let us consider each of these possibilities. The first, in which world order depends upon co-operation among national states, obviously contemplates a British victory in the present war and the re-establishment of pre-war boundaries—an outcome which daily appears less likely but which by some miracle might conceivably still come about. Under such circumstances the creation of a world order more stable than that prevailing before the war will require certain very drastic modifications of the institutional framework and international thinking with which we have been familiar.

The broad outline of these modifications has been indicated in the mimeographed memorandum we have been discussing during this Institute. They will be of three major types: those affecting the role of the national state; those affecting the role and character of international organization; and those affecting the attitudes of public opinion toward international affairs.

# A MORE STABLE WORLD ORDER

With respect to the modifications in the role of national states, a more stable world order will depend upon putting into practice in international relations the conception of the state as a means toward the improvement of the individual's welfare. This involves placing voluntary limitations upon the traditional sovereignty of states. Superficially, this means that no longer may the government of a national state judge its own case, defend its judgment by its own force alone, or refuse to be bound by changes in international law without its own consent. And it means further that no state may arbitrarily prevent access to its markets and raw materials by citizens of other states. It means, of course, the practical elimination of unlimited power from the means available to the national state to secure acceptance of its will. It means the establishment of some kind of international standard of human rights to be incorporated in the fundamental law of each state.

As the power of the national state is thus circumscribed, it will become possible and necessary materially to increase the scope of international machinery. This international machinery will need to be both universal and regional in order to allow adequately for the special interests of particular areas. It will have to have real power over matters affecting the settlement of international disputes and the imposition of effective sanctions for violations of international obligations. But it must also have power to legislate on those economic, political, and social matters which affect the interests of the nations under its jurisdiction and upon which peace depends. Probably more than any other single factor, the lack of this power of international legislation caused the breakdown of the League system. In this respect a new international organization must go well beyond the recommendations of the Bruce Committee,[4] which presupposed in its deliberations the continuation of national states with unlimited sovereignty. Into the details of all this organization it is unnecessary to go at this point, since so much time has already been devoted to it in our round tables. However, it should be emphasized that it will be no use planning for world organization unless that organization is to be universal or at least includes the important states. If the United States again intends to refuse responsibilities, it would be better not to try world organization at all.

The third modification suggested above concerns not the institutions themselves but the underlying attitude of people toward international affairs.

It is true that a great deal of the responsibility for the debacle of the last twenty years rests upon

[4] "Report of Special Committee: The Development of International Cooperation in Economic and Social Affairs," *League of Nations Publication A 23, 1939* (Geneva, 1939).

the shoulders of those men, living and dead, who deliberately risked the loss of our liberal democratic ideals, of our lives, and of world peace in order to further their own personal progress to political power. Some of these men were found in the victorious nations of Europe which were led to sacrifice the peace of other countries in order to retain the fruits of victory. Others were found in the United States, which was led by them to aid in the defeat of world organization, and we are only now awakening to the horrible costs (in national defense, economic distress, and possible war) of their political irresponsibility. Still others are found in those states which today appear to be on the road to world domination, but at costs to all mankind that can still not be even estimated.

Such irresponsible leadership is no mere accident. The real question is why these men should have been able to secure a following and how their equivalents in the future may be kept away from positions of influence. This raises two very fundamental issues, as far as the United States is concerned, not adequately considered in recent years. One concerns our educational practices; the other, our political organization.

Our educational pattern of thinking on world affairs is in need of a serious overhauling if effective international organization is to be made possible. The popular habit of mind which draws a sharp distinction between "international" affairs and "domestic" affairs is not merely due to the influence of the philosophy of nationalism, although this is a potent force here as elsewhere. It reflects also the failure of our educational methods to present a true picture of the modern world. The specialization within the social sciences which results in the teaching of separate courses on international politics and on international economics has served to perpetuate the myth that international political and economic questions can be isolated from national. Similarly, the segmentation of social knowledge among various social sciences has failed to prepare students adequately for the whole problems presented by an integrated world society. Moreover, in our universities, colleges, and secondary schools the teaching of international relations has too often been in terms of preachments on the brotherhood of man, the horrors of war, and the undesirability of using force under any circumstances. Too little attention has been given to the dynamics and realities of international relations as political issues in our industrial society.

Simultaneously with the overhauling of our thinking on world affairs in a formal educational sense there must be a quickening of the pace at which those no longer in the schools and colleges may be brought up to date—i.e., not merely in knowledge of what is happening day by day, but in knowledge of underlying principles for interpreting events. Only as this additional effort is made in the field of adult education can there be expectations of changing the policies which changing conditions require. (The degree to which the farmers of this country for many decades followed proponents of high industrial tariffs, and thus regularly made their own conditions worse, suggests how strenuous an effort has to be made to pry a people from outworn political beliefs, even when their best interests are involved.

The other basic issue concerns our political organization. If there is to be a prospect of making international organization effective, there must be changes in our political structure which will make it possible for the popular will in democracies to make itself felt. That this has not been true in the United States is evident when one considers that when a majority of the members of the United States Senate favored American membership in the League of Nations, it was possible for a handful of men who represented the margin necessary for a two-thirds majority to block the popular will. Again, when American opinion was so clearly favorable to our membership in world organization after the war that the Republican party found it necessary to seek "internationalist" sponsors for Warren G. Harding, the popular will was again blocked by a refusal of the successful party to carry out its implicit promises. All of this suggests the immediate need of an overhauling of the methods by which government in this country is supposed to be held in check by the people. It is obvious that a similar disparity between government policy and popular will exists on many occasions in other democratic states.

A mention of the shortcoming of the democratic system within national states is, however, not sufficient. If world organization is to be made to work the next time, there must be found means of representation in the international assembly which will make the spokesman in international discussions responsible to the people (not just to their governments) and make people feel a responsibility for what their spokesmen say. This question is closely related to the broader one of finding symbols of international loyalty comparable in strength to those which bind the national state. The implications of this statement are, I believe, clear and need not be spelled out at this point.

2. I turn now to the second possible political configuration which may face us at the end of this war—that of an order in the world based upon the domination of a single country in each of a limited number of areas. These areas might be Western Europe under Germany; Russia under the U.S.S.R.; the Far East under Japan; the Americas including Canada and Central and South America under the

leadership of the United States, with democratic axes extending out to Australia, New Zealand, and any other existing uncontrolled and democratic areas.

From an organizational point of view there are two sets of relations which will need to be considered. The first are the relations within each area. I think it need not be argued that in an area under the control of the present Nazi government the principle of organization will be domination by force rather than co-operation. There will be little occasion for applying the world's experiences in institutional co-operation, since independent sovereign states will exist only to the extent to which they conform to the centralized *Grossraumwirtschaft* of the imperial German state. This will be a problem of administrative organization and, in true fascist style, will have little in common with principles of co-operation, democratic responsibility, etc.

Correspondingly in Russia and the Far East there will be little occasion for facing problems of international organization, though one should observe that at least on paper the communist acceptance of federalism permits of somewhat more local autonomy than does centralized fascism under the Führer principle.

Within the American orbit there will very likely be ample opportunity to practice international or-

ganization. Even the nineteenth- and early twen-
tieth-century Latin-American policy of the United
States had elements of genuine co-operation in it,
and the more recent trends of our Latin-American
policy have been in the direction of greater equality and co-operation. Canada will no doubt want
to come into this system and will be encouraged to
do so. However, it is unlikely that the United
States will be blind to the time factor, which is all
important if the unity of a group of independent
states is to be preserved in the face of a highly organized, skilfully directed, and increasingly successful fascist method of expansion. Consequently,
it is to be expected that the unity of this hemisphere will be encouraged by all manner of democratic devices, but, if this proves too slow, whatever other methods are necessary will be employed
in the interest of our own defense.

In many respects the errors of the world as a
whole during the period 1920–40 can be easily repeated if the states of the American sphere, and
particularly the United States, insist upon all the
outworn rights of national sovereignty. There is a
real chance that what ultimately defeated the peace
efforts of the world and later destroyed so many
democratic states of Europe will also doom the independence and institutions of the New World.
There is in fact more danger in so far as the nation-
alist spirit is here more recent and in so far as the

direction of American trade and the depressed condition of agriculture and industry create fertile soil in which to sow seeds of discontent.

It is difficult at best to make the principle of world organization work on less than a world-wide basis, because of the forced dislocation of trade which is necessary and because of the competition for profits, loyalty, and political sympathy which comes from the outside. The United States must therefore recognize that far more than the kind of co-operation which would have been expected of it as a member of the League of Nations must be forthcoming to assure the success of the new American union of states. I believe that nothing short of the drastic modifications suggested above as essential for a new world-wide organization will be adequate to make union of the Americas of any value. The tariff policies of the United States must now be conceived in terms of the interests of the Americas and not of those who have concentrated political power in the United States, for the production of this hemisphere must be considered as a unit in relation to the products of the rest of the world. We shall need to prepare ourselves for large government purchases of Latin-American surpluses even if they must ultimately be burned. Such expenditures are as justifiably to be charged to national defense as the floating of cruisers. There must, therefore, be an inter-American economic planning board of some kind concerned with industrial and agricultural production, with transportation, and with credit facilities. Correspondingly, a greater body of American machinery for the handling of political and other disputes (within the Americas or with states elsewhere in the world), with power to compel conformance, will need to be devised at an early date. Not all these institutions can be immediately made operative, but the greatest of speed is necessary in that direction, and the United States must show generously that it means business.

The cartel now under construction may possibly be a step in this direction, as were Mr. Hull's many admirable efforts in behalf of American solidarity at recent inter-American conferences. Much of the League's experience should be drawn upon, and the use of some of its former personnel would seem to be indicated. From the Americas many men served in the League's Secretariat during the last twenty years. We should capitalize on their professional experience and international administrative knowledge.

I assume in the foregoing that opportunity will be provided for other countries not under fascist domination to join the economic and political union of the Americas.

With respect to the interregional relations and organizations which may develop, it may simply be suggested that these will probably be limited to the social-welfare machinery. This will for the time— at least until the issue between the Americas and the other regions has been more clearly drawn and settled—be limited to the more primitive ones. Until then it is impossible to predict to what extent the fascist governments will be willing to be bound by international obligations and under what conditions the United States would be ready to accept reciprocal obligations. It is to be expected that Germany will continue her support of the efforts to control the traffic in women and children and in dangerous drugs, and that she will want to aid in checking the spread of disease. Her one criterion of co-operation will likely be that the institutions shall in no way threaten the supremacy of the totalitarian national state. Should the present war end with a forcible Nazi victory in Europe, the stability of the world will depend largely upon the balance of power among the four great areas of control. It will not depend upon institutions of organized international co-operation.

No one so far removed from the final outcome of this world war should be very positive in his remarks about the kind of world organization we are going to see. I have limited myself to a consideration of those two of the possible situations we may face which appear to me to be most likely. Whether they are the only possibilities depends upon circumstances which are today wholly unpredictable. Could a victorious England withstand the domestic forces of change which are restless over the slowness of social reform and progress? Could a victorious Germany succeed in administering its vast new empire and could it convince the United States that appeasement can be profitable? These and many other questions must be answered before we can enter the blueprint stage of discussing international institutions after the war.

It may be said, however, with some degree of confidence, that out of the present world struggle will finally emerge a world order based upon one of two diametrically opposed conceptions of social organization. The one, the components of which are fairly clear from its history and our experience, will maximize freedom. It is a type of order which is the product of the relatively free interplay of the competitive forces of social life. The other, the components of which are equally clear from its most recent record and from its history in earlier times, represents an order maintained by power and domination. Upon the outcome of this struggle, which is but the most recent phase of an age-old conflict, will depend the character of the institutional framework required by the world order.

# INDEX

# INDEX

# INDEX

# INDEX